TOYO
ITO

TOYO ITO

Φ

7   In Search of a New Architectural Order
    Toyo Ito
21 The Amazing Mr Ito
    Dana Buntrock
26 Genesis and Evolution
    Taro Igarashi
30 The Discovery of Process
    Riken Yamamoto

68 TRANSPARENT WALLS

70 ITM Building in Matsuyama
74 T Building in Nakameguro

34 CAVE HOUSES

36 White U
40 House in Kasama

78 MUSEUMS

80 Yatsushiro Municipal Museum
84 Gallery U in Yugawara
88 Shimosuwa Municipal Museum

44 INCLUSIVE HOUSES

46 Silver Hut
52 House in Magomezawa

92 ROOFS WITH HOLES

94 Home for the Elderly in Yatsushiro
98 Yatsushiro Fire Station

56 UNHEAVY METAL

58 Tower of Winds in Yokohama
62 Egg of Winds
64 Restaurant Bar 'Nomad'

102 DOME

104 Odate Jukai Dome

110 THEATRES

    112   Nagaoka Lyric Hall
    116   T Hall in Shimane
    122   Matsumoto Performing Arts Centre

132 MEDIATHEQUE / LIBRARY

    134   Sendai Mediatheque
    144   Tama Art University Library (Hachioji campus)

156 PAVILIONS

    158   Bruges Pavilion
    162   Serpentine Gallery Pavilion 2002

166 ALUMINIUM STRUCTURES

    168   Aluminium Cottage
    172   Aluminium Brick Housing in Groningen
    176   Dormitory for SUS Company Fukushima Branch

184 URBAN NURTURE

    186   Hospital Cognacq-Jay in Paris

192 COMMERCIAL BUILDINGS

    194   TOD'S Omotesando Building
    202   MIKIMOTO Ginza 2

208 SPIRALS

    210   Relaxation Park in Torrevieja
    214   Island City Central Park 'GRIN GRIN'
    222   Meiso no Mori Municipal Funeral Hall

    229   Biography
    229   Project Data
    231   Index

In Search of a New Architectural Order

TOYO ITO

Architecture is the act of creating order

Houses once were built by people to protect themselves from the various dangers of the natural world. This attempt at securing a place to be, one that provided a stability that was impervious to the effects of the fluctuating conditions of the external world, was simultaneously also an act aimed at defining human relationships (such as those of the family) in terms of spatial order. In other words, what was required of a house from the very first stage of its historical emergence was the creation of a stable order that both defied external and obeyed internal conditions.

Since antiquity, humanity has endeavoured to give this stable order a clear form through diverse intellectual and technological developments. It could be said that the reason that the house as a dwelling-place came to be understood as 'architecture' was in the 'formalization of order' which integrated spatial composition, a framing system, and a correct response to the environment. For example, in terms of Japanese wooden buildings, from the primitive forms of pit dwelling to the refined forms of '*shoin-zukuri*' (one of Japan's most important residential architectural styles, dating from the sixteenth century) and teahouses, different historical periods saw the emergence of architectural conventions that were appropriate for the times, through the holistic combination of the manners and rules in social and everyday life, aesthetics and technology. The same goes for stonebuilt architecture, where the newly discovered technologies and structural and framing systems made possible by them, such as the arch or the dome, were subsequently used for different expressive purposes according to the dominant ideology of the period, thus inducing distinct architectural meanings in different periods.

Diverse architectural forms thus came to life through the conjunction of various factors such as meteorological conditions, existential conditions in relation to the external world, and the structural systems available at a certain period. These systems were also compositional in that they would also define the plan and the facade of the building. To construct architecture was therefore an act that depicted the holistic order encompassing the thoughts and sensibilities of a certain society in a certain historical period.

The element that has constantly played a crucial role in the process that defines this order is geometry. This was especially true in the West, where any act aimed at expressing order could never be dissociated with the strong sense of purity and completeness of the schema of Euclidean geometry. It is unsurprising that geometric forms with the highest sense of conclusiveness, such as the circle or the square, were valued in pursuit of the architectural expression of an order that was independent from the natural world.

The order of modernist architecture

The dramatic developments in construction methods in the twentieth century exemplified by the steel frame or reinforced concrete brought a significant change in architectural paradigms. The marked increase in world population and its concentration in urban areas after the industrial revolution made it imperative for urban architecture to expand in size, to verticalize, and to be industrially mass produced. The mass production of tridimensional grid-like architecture, in which columns, beams and floor slabs were sequentially placed horizontally and perpendicularly to each other, was a result of this necessity. Now all cities around the world present a strikingly similar urban landscape characterized by high-rise office buildings and apartments built in close succession.

Architecture originally used to be synonymous with the construction of a house in the sense of creating a stable place for dwelling. However, the advancement in our civilization caused houses to expand and workplaces to differentiate and specialize. Factories and stores also became independent, followed by office buildings.

When people lead a communal life, houses cluster together to form a settlement, which then expands and makes various functions independent to develop into a city. Those facilities we deem public today, such as the library, the auditorium, the museum, or even sports facilities and schools, all originally stemmed from the house and subsequently became differentiated and independent. It is therefore possible to think about the contemporary city that we live in as an extended house, however complex its structure may be. In this sense the city should in fact possess a constitutive principle or format, just as architecture does. Cities used to embody a clearly defined order. However, in cities the political and economic mechanisms of every historical period are physically accumulated and superimposed in layers, making it difficult to recognize a clear order.

We spend the majority of our everyday lives in tridimensional grid architecture. The places where we live, work, eat or play, in other words the places where we spend an unparalleled amount of time, are all situated in spaces constructed on this grid. The architectural order of the twentieth century could therefore be understood as that of the tridimensional grid.

This framework is aesthetically embodied in the images of Mies van der Rohe's steel and glass skyscrapers or Le Corbusier's concrete Unité d'habitation. These forms express a pure and abstract quality that can be referred back to Euclidean geometry, but they in fact present a contrasting set of meanings when compared to classical geometric expression. Whereas classical geometry emphasized a firmly static and completed order, the geometry of the grid expresses the potentially infinite expansion of a centreless space.

The transparent and homogeneous grid space was economical in terms of production and universal in terms of its versatility of use, and it was widely supported by city-dwellers, who sought free and non-hierarchical human relationships. Its usage continues to expand to the present day.

Is a new architectural order possible?

Contemporary society is controlled by the dominant logic of capital. Architecture too is on the verge of becoming a product of economy and information. New products, such as offices, apartments or hotels, can easily be produced one after another just by changing the surface of the grid's frame. This architectural form will continue to dominate contemporary society as long as the logic of capital remains unchanged.

The order of the grid assiduously amplifies the homogenization of space. This is because a homogeneous space ensures better economic efficiency and the provision of equal environmental conditions. However, the homogenization of space doesn't only go hand in hand with this characteristic of contemporary society – namely the homogenization of human relationships or even of society itself; there is also a synergetic effect. To put it succinctly, the grid is causing the homogenization of human beings.

Traditional wooden residential architecture retained a variation of different spaces within it, however small it may have been. This was due to the fact that its architectural forms were derived from environmental influences such as sunlight, wind and luminosity. An intimate relationship was maintained between nature and people, who responded to the differences in the spaces through the five senses.

Is it not alarming that people are letting the sharpness of their senses, in other words their animal instincts, degenerate under the order of a grid which cuts them loose from nature?

A further problem is posed by the impossibility of fundamentally solving the greatest issue of the twenty-first century, that of energy conservation, by continuing to utilize the homogeneous grid. The majority of the energy conservation measures now discussed are based on this homogeneous space, and rely on the production of an artificial environment with an ever-greater level of isolation from the external world achieved by improving the thermal insulation performance of the boundary that delimits the inside from the outside. It is hard to imagine any solution based on the idea of augmenting an internal artificial space (regardless of how much natural energy is used) leading to a departure from the doctrine of mechanical performance which has got us in this trouble in the first place.

We must recover an intimate relationship with the natural environment. Human beings were once a part of nature and so was architecture. Is it possible for us who live deeply immersed in the uniform spaces of the contemporary city to be reconciled with nature? Is it possible to recover the understanding of architecture as part of nature?

This issue may seem to have no easy solutions, but the corporal senses do significantly alter in relation to our consciousness of it. I believe that an instinctual yearning for contact with nature is constantly and latently present in us, and that even small stimuli could prompt it to manifest itself.

How, then, could architecture provide stimuli to this animal instinct? The first possibility that comes to mind is to transform homogeneous space.

For example, a rudimentary method could consist in inclining the lines that are parallel to the x, y and z axes of the grid in different directions. Those lines will no longer intersect orthogonally, but will do so in various obtuse and acute angles. The shapes engendered by the lines will no longer be solely square but also triangular or pentagonal. Even this kind of elementary manipulation can bring about an inhomogeneous and unstable space unknown in the language of the grid pattern, and induce a certain sense of tension in the people using the space. By making the lines curved, the heterogeneity of the space could be further accentuated, or in other words a soft instability would arise.

However, as much as these series of manipulations based on bending, distorting and creating non-orthogonal intersections would be successful in generating inhomogeneous spaces, they could not generate a new order. It would perhaps be more accurate to understand them as actions taken to dismantle an existing order.

What kind of method could be employed for an inhomogeneous or unstable order to be generated? The answer lies in biological organisms in the natural world. Humanity developed its classical geometric shapes and grid spaces by seeking an absolute order against the world of natural phenomena, a world of animals and plants regarded as having no conceivable order because of its constant repetition of the cycle of fluid growth, decay and death. What today attracts our attention most compellingly is exactly this fluid order in nature that constantly grows and changes. The fact that there are fundamental rules that generate all the living manifestations of the universe is now being clearly revealed in various fields of the biological sciences.

The most prominent characteristic of living organisms is the fact that their order is not absolute. The conformity of things may reach a certain balance in one particular instant, but in the next moment it transforms into a different one. This order is relative, flexible and soft. It is a constantly and dynamically repeated self-organization.

Let us think about a tree as the most easily comprehensible example of such a flexible order. The final form of a tree is a highly complex one despite the fact that its growth is based on the simple rule of one limb branching out into two. Each tree is unique even amongst the same tree species, due to the balance each attains through negotiation with its internal and external environments. A constant process of autogenic growth can be observed in their gradual change.

To generate order by setting a basic rule such as the one found in a tree's growth, and allowing various external factors to interact with this rule: Would this not be the correct method to attain a new architectural order based on instability and heterogeneity?

An 'algorithm' could be defined as a rule that correctly generates a complex and unstable, but at the same time soft and highly flexible, order. It is an internal rule which, in relation to the various parameters that are added to it, heterogeneously determines how the architectural organization of forms will be externalized. Any algorithmic method must of necessity be a non-linear process that changes every second in accordance with changes in external conditions. The result is always non-invertible: that is to say, the process always leads to unknown results.

An algorithmic architectural order thus closely approximates the order of the natural world. Presently, the algorithms that are utilized in architectural design are still in their primitive stages, but there is no doubt that they will generate spatial structures that have little to do with those of the grid architecture of the twentieth century. There is equally no doubt that if architecture comes to approximate the system of living organisms in the natural world even slightly, people's basic bodily sensations would be awakened. I think we should create architecture that makes people happy, cheerful and more energetic, taking at the same time a significant step towards a humane solution to the issues posed by the global environment.

← Page 6:
Foyer area (Matsumoto Performing Arts Centre)

→ Following pages:
View of the roof (Meiso no Mori Municipal Funerary Hall)
Exterior view (MIKIMOTO Ginza 2)
View toward the street from the stairs (TOD'S Omotesando Building)
Aerial view (White U)
Inside of the west passage to the concert hall (Nagaoka Lyric Hall)
View of the structure from the interior (Serpentine Pavilion)
View from across pond (Island City Central Park 'GRIN GRIN')
A tube under construction (Sendai Mediatheque)

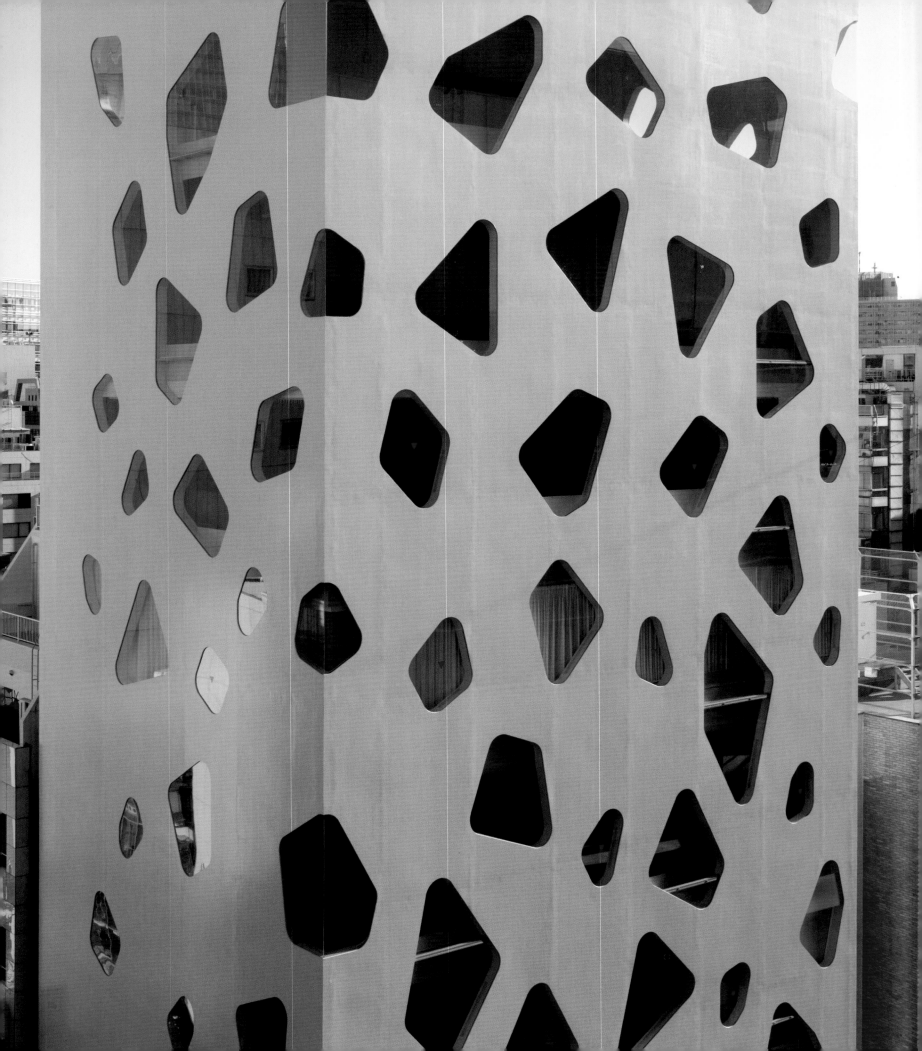

The Amazing Mr Ito

DANA BUNTROCK

Like ice flows the solid is at risk.
Cecil Balmond[1]

Ito seemed to continually be saying 'pow'.
Ray Ryan[2]

Have you ever seen magic? A slim figure stands on a vast, empty stage, the surrounding space underscoring that he works alone, implying there is no tricky paraphernalia. An assistant rolls in something heavy like a huge Humvee and the conjurer levitates it into the air, offers a soft smile and then, with the wave of a white handkerchief, makes it disappear. Or perhaps the conjurer invites someone from the audience to join him up on stage – and the unwitting recruit is suddenly staring across that big space at her own feet, clearly cleaved from her body, wiggling her toes with a look of more-than-mild surprise on her face.

It is interesting how often photographers isolate Toyo Ito's slender frame against something like an ample expanse of unadorned concrete or a wide white plaster wall, as if emphasizing he, too, is apparently alone. Ito works magic. He once wrote that he was attempting to achieve 'a house as light as cloth, fluttering in the air … a town where clothes, furniture, *paos,* and houses are all fluttering in the wind like sinuous clothes … The entire town, swaying and glowing …'[3] He spent years perfecting his ability to make a building float, fabric-like. He started by suspending a perforated aluminium (unfortunately uninhabitable) 'electronic tent', the Pao II, at an exhibition in Brussels in 1989, then ultimately succeeded with substantial slabs of steel at the airy, open interiors of his 2001 Sendai Mediatheque. You might think he worked that magic alone, but the remarkable latticed tubes and beam-free floor at Mediatheque resulted from an at-the-time unusually rich collaboration with the esteemed engineer Mutsuro Sasaki. The photographer Naoya Hatakeyama froze this moment on film as a crucial turning point in Ito's career, a lush drape of white welding curtains fringed in rust wrapping one of Ito's audacious tubes like theatre curtains poised before the play.

Remember when structural engineers seemed dull and earthbound, cluttering up architects' efforts at an idealized open space with annoying K-braces? No more. Another who achieves equally exciting results when working with Ito, UK-based Cecil Balmond, enjoys the challenge, too. He contended that the Japanese architect's work today 'does not seem to sit on the ground … it slides and flows, and the eye is engaged always by the movements, slow or fast, angled or undulating'.[4] The architect could not achieve his effects without someone like this Arup engineer, two professionals together coming up with increasingly outrageous, seemingly implausible tricks.

Having mastered the illusion of lightness, Toyo Ito proceeded to make his pavilion at Bruges in 2002 disappear.

(Or nearly so – the aluminium has been beefed up a bit, because otherwise the whole thing would have been too imperceptible to enjoy.) Working with still another skilful structural engineer, Tokyo's Masato Araya, he stiffened the sides of this tunnel-like slice of space with playful planar polka-dots most people might easily overlook as simple, ornamental embellishments. But without those dots, the honeycomb that makes up the pavilion drooped alarmingly. The most interesting photographs of the pavilion's early stages portray Ito's youthful staff standing in the garage beneath his office, an outrageous deflection in the half-scale section they are shoring up with their hands. The kids are laughing at the absurdity – this sagging structure is going to be a building? Who will hold it up, when it is erected on the other side of the world? They surely did not yet expect the ethereal end result of their efforts.

And our bodies? Long before most understood we would be chatting with friends across sea and space via tiny phones carried in our pockets, Ito was exploring the social implications of severing our bodies into two, one visceral and sensual, the other inhabiting the ether. Almost everyone puzzled over his musings, his cryptic comments that we were Tarzans in a media forest. We thought ourselves sophisticates, when we were about to become unaware pioneers in an uncharted and unchartable place. Ito understood the implications of the emerging tiny technologies in our hands, saw that they both challenged and enriched our social networks with virtual ones.

On the stages of nineteenth-century Europe, magic was an art of mathematics, too. Ito and Cecil Balmond engage in these intellectually elegant tricks: at the Serpentine Pavilion in London, they spun squares into smaller squares, concealing their geometry in a complicated pattern that reveals itself only upon inspection. Balmond is inclined to mathematic riddles, but Ito drew out of the engineer an unusual exquisiteness by insisting this rigour yield randomness. Elsewhere, Ito explores other algorithms: spiralling Bezier curves shelter an uncluttered open space at the Relaxation Park in Torrevieja, Spain; towers twist at Barcelona's Gran Via Trade Fair campus; and his Taichung, Taiwan, Opera House, as yet unbuilt and seemingly unbuildable, is based on a mind-bending torus-based set of cells. Ito proposed that idea initially in 2004 for a competition, the Ghent Forum for Music, Dance and Visual Culture, in an intense collaboration with Araya and the Milanese architect Andrea Branzi. The team was enormously emboldened by a juror's exhortations for proposals that would turn theatre on it head – but became aware too late that these comments were, as they too often are in architecture, more rhetoric than reality.

All that emptiness, that airy ethereality in Ito's architecture, is far from easy. It requires elaborate preparation. A magician does not work unaided; the stage is often wrapped in a wizardry of apparatus, the irrational in front of our eyes resulting from a very up-to-date understanding of technology and science. Nineteenth-century conjurers used

Designed for a performance of *The Marriage of Figaro* for junior-high school students, Ito's 2005 stage set was a knot of veneer plywood stretching 24 metres from the deepest reaches of the performance area, cascading into the orchestra pit, and ending at the first row of spectator seats.

unseen electro-magnets to shift the apparent weight of steel-bottomed boxes at a time when those in the audience did not yet understand such forces. In the same way, Ito wrapped the tube-like stairs of Sendai Mediatheque in fire-resistant glass when few even knew yet that it existed. For his 2005 Mikimoto tower, he slipped concrete into a steel sandwich, stiffening the exterior envelope so that it acted as an unseen, fire-resistant structure, a subtler, perhaps more permanent version of those playful polkadots. Advances in computer technology also allow the architect to craft improbably thin, structurally-optimized billowing slabs, as Ito did at the 2006 Meiso no Mori Municipal Funerary Hall in Kakamigahara, a concrete cloud.

Magicians have an interest in tension; at least one advises aspiring presdigitators to give greater thought to gravity, asserting that tautness in a muscle can undermine a trick. Ito is also inclined to suppress stress and strain, intending an effortless appearance. His engineers employ sophisticated softwares to illuminate weaknesses embedded in an initial idea; columns of colourful graphics illustrate iterations that initially include dangerously red and yellow sections of structure, increasingly adjusted to a pacific blue and green in the final, most efficient outcomes.

Earlier Ito explored optics and light, the stagecraft of illusionists. The abstract air of the U-shaped interior in a 1976 house, designed for his musicologist sister in her mourning, was enhanced by elongated shadows cast from footlights. (The idea emerged while tippling with plasterers at the end of the working day.) He designed lighting for an Opera House in Frankfurt in 1991 and stage sets, including the three luminous, twisting tubes for the dance group Fluid Hug Hug (a name Ito conceivably might have adopted for

his own office, had he started out today). The architect also designed a sinuous setting for the *Marriage of Figaro* in 2005; Ito now uses stage sets as he once did installations, to isolate and exaggerate his intriguing ideals. Yet Ito's theatrical interiors, while demonstrating his skilful handling of light and sight, are often surprisingly conventional spatially. This seems to be the consequence of nervous clients like those at Ghent, who fear deviating too far from the norms for such settings; even the insistently avant-garde design now under development for the University of California, Berkeley, Art Museum holds at it heart two surprisingly stereotypical cinema spaces. Perhaps, though, the open arrangements in the proposed Taichung Opera House will uncover other opportunities for Ito to innovate more aggressively in this arena.

Ito has been encouraged to be splendidly adventurous elsewhere. He made sound and breeze visible at his 1986 Tower of Winds, feeding information about intensity into a computer program that played lights across the perforated panels of its skin. He made its concrete shaft transparent and dainty; he argued he could render the built world 'fictional' or 'fickle' in this way. Ito washed floors and walls in a dizzying blur of projected imagery at exhibitions such as the 1991 'Visions of Japan' in London, where the Crown Prince, who came all the way from Tokyo, longed for a glass of sake to enhance the experience. Charles Jencks wrote that at this exhibition, 'the observer felt he had intruded accidentally inside someone's brain to float between firing neurons and exploding holograms. The effect was mesmerizing, hypnotic, disorienting, intoxicating. … I found spectators lost in a trance … the old-time Archigrammer, Ron Herron, sitting cross-legged on the floor, soaking in this electronic nirvana.'[5] The American academic Kenneth Frampton observed that Ito's 'dramatic effect evokes the illusory changes suffered by the protagonists of Lewis Carroll's famous tale, with the rabbit disappearing into the darkness and Alice continually experiencing a marked instability with regard to size'.[6] Ito seemed to offer up two architectures at the time: the dizzying digital forecasts of our future were mechanically and technologically finicky, in fact, so his permanent structures strove instead for an empty simplicity in order to achieve ephemerality. The influence of that era's experiments endures; even now, Ito retains a fascination for glass, mirrors, and shiny surfaces, for making walls seem to slip away as the light shifts or reflections double depth, evident in his cascading voids at the heart of the otherwise understated Mahler 4 building in Amsterdam, completed in 2005.

Ito has always held higher ambitions than simply making buildings appear unstable, proposing, 'In some conceptual reality[,] we can think of such an ideal of architecture within which Paris can be turned on and off.'[7] Reading this remark in the post-9/11 world where we live today, switching a city off seems somehow more credible and chilling. This may be the reason others sometimes see disturbing darkness in

Ito's output, while he himself insistently argues he is an under-appreciated optimist. Ito was and is more interested in temporarily turning on simulacra of cities in new spaces than in extinguishing their originals.

Ito's interest in the digital realm extends to contraptions. He first called his office 'Urban Robot', because it was intended as a partnership with IT expert Yoshio Tsukio, who programmed Arata Isozaki's amusingly cartoonish automatons at the 1970 Osaka Expo.[8] Nearly twenty years later, Ito invited electronic artist Anthony Dunne to add 'unpacked television sets' and 'comical androids that breathe the air of information' to the already cacophonous liquid crystal-lined 'Visions of Japan' installation; in response to these cute cyborgs, onomatopoetically entitled *bombom, hyoro, pukupuku, dandan* and *guruguru,* Ito argued, 'Are we not becoming like these objects? … without us realizing it, our bodies are turning into androids.'[9] Us, electronically enhanced. The Spanish architect Elias Torres insightfully suggested Ito is in possession of gadgets many architects would envy: a column space extruder, a liquid transparency filter, a sky cutter, and a light brush. Torres also illustrates exquisite implements only Ito would wield: musical wind scissors, perfume catching spray, and a glass wings beater.

Magicians are notorious for intensively scrutinizing their rivals' performances, for trading tricks only grudgingly. They have no intention of explaining their most costly innovations; ingenious apparatus is employed for years. The construction and engineering of Ito's recent architecture is no small trick; if you have experience in the field, it is hard not to want to look closer, to try to understand his curving steel or shotcrete. Architects around the world struggle to decipher Ito's engineering of late. Greenhorns and geeks flock to his construction sites at every chance – thousands toured Sendai Mediatheque during its erection, and I have seen many high-end cocktail parties less crowded than the day they showed off the Mikimoto construction site to friends and family. (The contractor concealed a trick from me there, refusing to explain how they so neatly welded the panels in place when starting from each corner and working inward – that's the way they assured that nice straight edge on each end of the facade.) Ito, however, is not dependent on hiding his technology; he happily annotates each unusual structure of late in its subsequent publication, including engineering diagrams and fabrication photos.

In part, this is because the architect does not revisit a tactic twice. Ito admits, 'Most of the projects we have done since Sendai have been very likely unrepeatable … all incredibly demanding operations.'[10] And in truth, his audience does not allow him to play the same hand again, aware that even the best trick loses its thrill on repetition. Early texts on stagecraft advised making artefacts disappear in a variety of ways in order to increase the awe; Ito nimbly explores new inventions in each entirely unique structure. Latticed steel tubes and beam-free floors at Sendai were followed by the aluminium honeycomb at Bruges. The forest

Elias Torres's charming collage of Ito's tricky tools includes a 'column space extruder' created from Sendai Mediatheque's tubes (upper right); a knife-like 'liquid transparency fixer' (left), its handle made from lobby seating in the Nagaoka Lyric Hall; a 'sky cutter' blade rendered from the wing-like roof of the Yatsushiro Municipal Museum (right), and a 'light brush' crafted from the banded ceiling at, again, Sendai Mediatheque (bottom right corner).

of trees at the 2004 boutique for TOD'S shoes was represented with paper – appropriate, as the almost paper-thin self-consolidating concrete wall is 28 cm of lace holding up seven floors. His trees re-emerged in proposals for Musashino outside Tokyo, and Amiens (both remain unbuilt). Instead, at the 2007 Tama University Library, a related steel and concrete structure is a more open, seismically resistant Swiss cheese of oddly syncopated arches.

In the same fashion, it might be argued that the cast glass and precast concrete skin at the 2004 Matsumoto Performing Arts Centre is a precedent for the rippling surface proposed for S Project in Scotland, and this then subsequently led to an unfortunately anaemic arrangement at the VivoCity shopping mall in Singapore, draped in Ductal concrete. The undulating canopies at 'GRIN GRIN' in Fukuoka, in truth both annoyingly hairy and oddly appealing, owe something to the Meiso no Mori Municipal Funerary Hall and the Relaxation Park in Torrevieja. Even while each structure remains unique, there are families of ideas in Ito's overall *oeuvre.*

Interestingly, Ito asserted Balmond is the magician, producing an 'endless string of sketched ideas out of his bag' – but the Japanese architect is equally adept at this.[11] Publications today share small slices of the innumerable iterations his staff offer up. The office spins space out of a variety of structural materials and systems, fine-tuning exhaustively, interrogating engineers, contractors and fabricators – indeed, anyone who might offer an answer – on how to achieve their ideals. But an avid interest in unusual engineering would only attract nerdy folks trying to figure out how the architect and Araya got all that re-bar into the crucial corners at TOD'S or to understand the effort

Toyo Ito as the King of Diamonds in a pack of playing cards designed by Taro Igarashi and Akira Asada

involved in constructing Sasaki's counter-weighting cantilevered tiers for the balconies of the Matsumoto Performing Arts Centre. Magic appeals to the child in all of us, although perhaps a bit more so to those educated enough to understand its improbability.

Yet people who clearly have no interest in avant-garde architecture interact in delight with Ito's work. Who went to his 2006 'The New Real', an exhibition of construction drawings and concrete formwork? Children and grannies. They ignored the full-scale building sections drawn on the wall, of course – they simply played in the pits Ito cut into his billowing, fleshy floor, and cavorted on the sullied concrete formwork of the crematorium. Can you imagine? I keep finding codgers sunning themselves in his sleek spaces, toddlers racing through his most serious structures, sweethearts nestled in odd corners of his elusively ordered institutions.

And here, in truth, is where Ito is really engaging in a sleight of hand. Magic is the art of concealing when apparently revealing, slyly distracting with an elegant gesture in an area unrelated to the most important action. Ito's magic is not in fact in the innovative and almost impossible engineering; it is in the spaces of his architecture today, in his acute observation of social behaviour. Ito knows how to make people want to hang out, argues that a public role for architecture is more important at a time when it is far from necessary. He is no longer as interested in our android selves, worrying instead about the increasing unimportance of our primitive and sensual side. This is not, in fact, a new concern. In his 1991 explication of the life of Tokyo's nomadic woman, Ito concluded her day poignantly: 'After wandering around in the city, the woman eventually comes back to her apartment and quietly sips coffee by herself. *This is the most fragile moment of reality for her.*'[12]

Oddly, he discovered one way to achieve his ends was to stop making what we might conventionally consider architecture. While executing the Sendai Mediatheque, paring the structure down to its simplest elements, Ito began alluding to it as 'infrastructure'. Soon after he produced what might be considered an odd manifesto for an architect:

a desire not to create joints
a desire not to create beams
a desire not to create walls
a desire not to create rooms
a desire not to create architecture.[13]

His spaces became larger, like urban streets, unadorned, and open to alteration by the events that occur within. Ito argued early on, 'If we compare the architecture of Western civilization to a museum, Japanese architecture is like a theatre. It provides various architectural elements, which are put together to form a stage where an event is to take place, rather than being there permanently … When the spectators have gone, all that is left is empty space.'[14] Even though he is extraordinarily skilful at the formalism so important to the critical community, when Ito eschewed aesthetic devices he finally discovered the spatial effects that have intrigued and eluded him for so long. His architecture became the invisible stuff, embodied, if you will, in its empty space.

Ito observed an initial low-key opening of the Sendai Mediatheque shortly after midnight on 1 January 2001. 'Young couples,' he recalled, 'walked around the building, touched, or had pictures taken in front of, the tubes. And then left in twos and threes … people experiencing the building for the first time seemed … as if they were out strolling on the street and not inside a building.'[15] This is Ito's ideal: small groups, families, lovers, drifting through his aqueous environments like exotic fish. Koji Taki, a philosopher who has been most accomplished at shining a light on Ito's ambitions, points out, 'Nation-states are not the issue for Ito, neither are socio-economic affairs at large of much interest. What does matter to him is how human life and spirit are faring in today's world; he's an avid observer.'[16] Ito is quite aware architects are expected to be elitist and intellectual, that 'they have worn their rejection by mainstream society like a badge of honour'.[17] To do so, however, would be to deny what he himself enjoys. Modern magicians play plebeian Las Vegas. In his younger days, Ito sometimes cited Tokyo's equally outré entertainment areas, seedy hotspots and honky-tonks he, too, frequented: Kabukicho, portrayed in the kaleidoscopic wash of images playing over the liquid crystal-lined walls and floor in 'Visions of Japan'; Shibuya, hunting grounds for the untethered Tokyo woman who inhabited his *pao;* raucous Roppongi, the site of his design for a shortlived bar named 'Nomad', an interior intended to recall a circus tent. 'I believe,' Ito asserted then, 'only in the pleasure of the moment.'[18]

At times today Ito allows himself to undercut the seriousness of architecture with a calmer, quirky humour. Like many Japanese architects, he designs objects – the oddest, perhaps, his dishware for Alessi, which produced tea sets in 2003 in limited, artwork-like editions of a thousand each, working with an international elite and the prestigious Max Protetch Gallery. Predictably, almost all explored abstraction, which Ito himself did not ignore; the flat faces of his plates and saucers achieve an uncompromising purity. But Ito also added an oddball embellishment, cute tiny green frogs clinging to his perfect porcelains. Surely it is this openness to amusement that led Japanese academics Taro Igarashi and Akira Asada to depict the architect as they did: the King of Diamonds in a pack of playing cards, dressed in a court jester's motley clothes. The 1991 Yatsushiro Museum is on his head; a frill from the Serpentine Pavilion is a collar, pinned with a shape reminiscent of the plan for his 'White U'; the Tama Art Library makes up his torso; and a leg-like latticed tube is in his hand. Jesters used quicksilver levity to undermine accepted fallacies – witty, well-spoken, erudite, non-conformist, musical and acrobatic. A lot like Ito.

Kenneth Frampton once argued that Ito's architecture offered an acerbic opposition to populism. I am far less sure of this today. That Ito is able to offer elegant abstraction is undeniable. That he is insightful, a visionary who saw our futures shining on the surfaces of still waters, is undeniable. But to encompass both popular appeal and intellectual inquiry, to be playful while wielding sparkling scientific skill, these are perhaps not as antithetical as our critical community insists. Ito's greatest feat today is that he is unafraid to be out of step, feeling freed from the pressure to perform because of his smashing success at Sendai. His mind-bending rejection of architectural aristocracy's anti-social inclinations will in the end be more important than the fact that, for the moment, only the amazing Mr Ito and his extraordinary engineers appear able to bend spoons of steel.

1   Cecil Balmond, 'Network', *Serpentine Gallery Pavilion 2002: Toyo Ito with Arup* (Tokyo 2002)
2   Ray Ryan, 'Star of the Silver Screen', *L.A. Architect* (March 1990), p. 5
3   Toyo Ito, 'House in Magomezawa, 1985, and Nomad Pub, Tokyo, 1986', *Architectural Design*, vol. 58, no. 5/6 (1988), p. 66
4   Cecil Balmond, 'Learning Ito', *Toyo Ito: The New 'Real' in Architecture* (Tokyo 2006), p. 24
5   Charles Jencks, 'Toyo Ito: Stealth Fighter for a Richer Post-Modernism', *Toyo Ito (Architectural Monographs No. 41)* (London 1995), p. 12
6   Kenneth Frampton, 'Ukiyo-e and the Art of Toyo Ito', *Space Design [SD]*, 8609, p. 145
7   'Avant Space: The Architectural Experiments of Toyo Ito', *World Architecture*, 34 (1995), p. 101
8   Noriko Takiguchi, *Nihon no Kenchikuka: Ito Toyo, Kansatsuki [Toyo Ito: Architect, Japan]* (Tokyo 2006), pp. 78 – 9
9   Toyo Ito, 'Architecture in a Simulated City', Andrea Maffei, ed., *Toyo Ito: Works, Projects, Writings* (Milan 2001), p. 334 Originally published in *Kenchiku Bunka* in 1991, a slightly different version of this essay can also be found at www.aec.at/en/archives/festival_archive/festival_catalogs/festival_artikel.asp?iProjectID=8677
10   Toyo Ito, 'The New "Real": Toward Reclaiming Materiality in Contemporary Architecture', *Toyo Ito: The New 'Real' in Architecture* (Tokyo 2006), p. 40
11   Toyo Ito, 'Architecture or Non-Architecture? The Architect and the Engineer', *Casabella*, 711 (2003), p. 109
12   Toyo Ito, 'Floating Pao in the Stream', *Columbia Documents of Architecture and Theory: D, 5* (1996), p. 107 The essay is a partial transcript of a 1991 lecture. My emphasis.
13   Quoted in Hera van Sande, *Toyo Ito Builds the Bruges 2002 Pavilion* (Oostkamp 2002), p. 5. The quotation is also used in Toyo Ito, 'Dividing vs. Making', *Toyo Ito: Sendai Mediatheque 1995–2000 (GA Detail 2)* (Tokyo 2000), p. 5, published there in a numbered list with punctuation.
14   Sophie Roulet and Sophie Soulie, 'Towards a Post-ephemeral Architecture: Interview with Toyo Ito', *Toyo Ito* (Paris 1991), p. 105
15   Toyo Ito, 'The Lessons of Sendai Mediatheque', *Japan Architect*, 41 (Spring 2001), p. 6
16   Koji Taki, 'Life and Technology', *Toyo Ito: The New 'Real' in Architecture* (Tokyo 2006), p. 12
17   Toyo Ito, 'A Body Image Beyond the Modern: Is There Residential Architecture without Criticism?', Andrea Maffei, ed., *Toyo Ito: Works, Projects, Writings* (Milan 2001), pp. 348 – 9
18   'Towards a Post-Ephemeral Architecture,' p. 93

Genesis and Evolution

TARO IGARASHI

*The Original
Fluid Landscape*

The place where Toyo Ito grew up was in the mountains in Nagano prefecture, by Lake Suwa. Facing on to this lake, his work, the Akahiko Memorial Hall in the Suwako Museum (1993), gently curves, forming a long, horizontal arc like a boomerang. For Ito, this work constituted one of the turning points away from austere modernistic form and towards the fluid design that characterized his works after the 1990s. The Matsumoto Performing Arts Centre (2004) that is situated in a nearby provincial city is also a music hall that sinuously extends along a narrow strip of land. Ito's image of forms reminiscent of flowing amorphous water may have come to life out of this juvenile landscape, I thought when I visited Lake Suwa. Ito has mentioned that he used to look at Lake Suwa every day on his way to school. It was not until he reached his fifties, however, and long after he began to work as an architect, that he arrived at the new direction in his design, as if he were going back to his origins.

A comparison with an architect born in the same prefecture, Terunobu Fujimori, proves interesting. He began his design activity after becoming well known as an architectural historian. His first work in Chino, the Jinch[o]gan Moriya Data Hall (1991), presents an eerie anomal form where columns burst through the eaves. Behind it, the treehouse Takasugi-an (Too-high Teahouse) (2004) floats 6 metres above the ground, and there are plans for building the Hikusugi-an (Too-low Teahouse) next to it by digging into the ground. Fujimori's vertical axis contrasts Ito's horizontal axis. Growing up in the surrounding mountain villages, Fujimori may have been influenced by the Onbashira Festival at the Suwa Taisha Shrine. His recent research that focuses on ancient standing stones and tree worship can be understood as a return to his own primordial landscape. The Moriya family itself has been responsible for the rituals at the Suwa Taisha Shrine for generations, and at the Data Hall designed by Fujimori they exhibit the history of the festivals. Fujimori's architecture revives the dynamism of antiquity in the present, just like the turbulent Onbashira Festival where logs are dropped down steep slopes.

On a related note, there has been an intriguing Shinto ritual enacted in Lake Suwa since at least the fourteenth century: the 'Omiwatari'. The surface of the lake freezes in winter. As the ice expands and contracts due to the difference in temperature from day to night, it cracks, accompanied by a roaring sound, giving rise to a 30–180 cm high mountain range of ice that stretches from one shore to the other. It is a landscape reminiscent of land art created by contemporary artists such as Robert Smithson or Michael Heuser. This is called 'Omiwatari' in Lake Suwa. According to legend, it is the route that the god Takeminakatanomikoto of the Suwa Upper Shrine passed through to meet the goddess Yasakatomenomikoto of the Lower Shrine. The first line that appears on the north–south axis and the next one that appears along the same axis after a few days are called, respectively, 'Ichi-no-owatari' (First Passage) and the 'Ni-no-owatari' (Second Passage), while the line that begins to form from the east shore and orthogonally intersects with the other two is called the 'Saku-no-owatari' (the Passage of Saku). These lines are visited in a ritual where the directions of the Owatari are inspected to perform an augury to predict the year's harvest.

Irregularly-shaped lines generated by natural meteorological phenomena. A protruding crack in ice creates an unexpectedly beautiful form. The dynamic sculpting of ice which takes place, appropriately, in Ito's native Lake Suwa, seems to indicate the direction that Ito strives towards in order to achieve a new geometry.

A water-like fluidity is not only noticeable in Ito's design, but also in his working attitude. Ito creates his architecture by forming a large vortex involving diverse people out of whom he draws particular talents, rather than by unilaterally imposing his own way. He enables a new architecture based on a network and communication amongst innumerable people. In her book documenting the two most important contemporary architects in the age of globalism, namely Ito and Rem Koolhaas, journalist Noriko Takiguchi describes the two as being diametrically opposed: 'Koolhaas, the aggressive, and Ito, the defensive who diverts the things that fall upon him to a different current.'[1] Here again a fluid image is noticeable. Ito himself asserts, 'I always think at least once whether I can alter my thinking at all by accepting the criticism of others … I always think about the possibility that my way of thinking may evolve by introducing the opinion of others.'[2] If Koolhaas is a ferocious carnivore, then Ito is a gentle herbivore.

Another point of interest regarding the image of water arises from an Ito text of fundamental importance and which is tantamount to a declaration of intent, 'There is No New Architecture Without Being Immersed in the Sea of Consumption,'[3] written in 1989, when Japan bustled with a bubble economy and postmodern architecture was prevalent. He believed that it was unproductive to mourn the loss of reality from the standpoint of conservative value judgement in an era where architecture was consumed and downgraded to the level of fashion or games. 'I believe,' he stated, 'that reality does not come before consumption but exists only beyond it, on the other side of consumption. This is why the only method for us possible in front of the sea of consumption, is to immerse ourselves in it and swim to the opposite shore to discover something.' Not to drown in the sea of consumption, but to face it and 'uncompromisingly question the possibility of achieving architecture'. Without a doubt, Ito has swum through the sea of the bubble economy, succeeded in a further development and arrived at the opposite shore: the 'new real'.

Informatization and the Image of Nature

It is probably possible to explain the conditions after 1990 by replacing the term 'consumer society' in Ito's declaration with 'information-based society'. This is Ito's fundamental approach: to seek new possibilities for architecture when it plunges into the crisis of the era of information. The 1990s saw the diffusion of computers and the mounting popularity of virtual or cyber architecture where people played with alterations in shape on a screen. In the actual city, equally, there appeared shipping-storage-like convenience stores connected to network apparatuses and commercial facilities with large screens displaying information, prompting speculation that 'architecture' might even disappear. True, what is called the 'information space' is difficult to visualize. A new technology kills architecture. Victor Hugo once said that the book will kill the edifice; is the computer going to eliminate architecture? Ito provided his negative answer by introducing the possibilities allowed by the computer into his design, thus reviving architecture.

The inauguration of the Sendai Mediatheque was striking. As the countdown towards the new millennium on the evening of 31 December reached zero, the glass door was opened and countless people rolled into the building. The Mediatheque was opened on 1 January 2000, in conjunction with the event for celebrating the coming of the new millennium. As if to symbolize the opening of a new era for architecture. In the competition which employed the term 'mediatheque' for the first time for a public facility in Japan, competitors were required to present a new archetype for the information era. Ito won this by presenting a model based on tubes, skin and plates as a substitute for traditional elements such as columns and walls.

In a symposium organized by the Nederlands Architectuur-instituut in Rotterdam in 2000 where Ito gave a lecture, a member of the audience pointed out that the Sendai Mediatheque was reminiscent of the architecture of Antonio Gaudí. The curvaceous sculptural quality in Gaudí's architecture, that while pursuing structural possibility is covered in ornamental elements, does in fact evoke physical sensations. Ito's transparency, however, fundamentally changes the impression of the architecture. Gaudí is an architect of the era of Spanish Modernismo, that is to say of Art Nouveau. It is interesting to compare the Art Nouveau which swept Europe around 100 years before the birth of the Sendai Mediatheque to the conditions of the present.

Art Nouveau literally aimed to achieve a 'new art'. It was a critique against nineteenth-century architecture which preoccupied itself solely with the arbitrary use of the catalogued styles of the past without considering the possibilities of the modern age. Art Nouveau appeared on the stage as the forefront of an avant-garde that sought to detach itself from historical elements. This was, of course, before modernism formulated a method for architectural design. Art Nouveau sought inspiration from nature or plants full of the energy of life. In fact, in Japan it is also known as 'the style of the flower'.

Terunobu Fujimori, Too-High Treehouse, Chino, 2004

The Sendai Mediatheque also refers to plant-like images. Famously, a single sketch was the beginning of the project. The idea that flashed into Ito's mind in an airport on January 1995 was of 6 columns wiggling inside a transparent box. It is difficult to immediately identify it as an architectural sketch. The image was of seaweed undulating in an aquarium, as the footnote 'seaweed-like columns' suggests. Nature was the inspiration.

According to Ito, the Sendai Mediatheque is a space like a forest. The mesh of tubes produced by welding steel pipes is reminiscent of trees and echoes the line of zelkova trees in front of the building. The homogeneity of the space is disturbed by the introduction of tubes. He creates diverse spaces by using nature as his foothold. No two places can be the same in the forest, where space is ordered by trees. Ito describes the Sendai Mediatheque as 'a layered urban forest. It is architecture, a forest, of intellect.'[4] At the turn of the century, it was nature again that inspired the architect.

Art Nouveau was born at a time when architecture was in crisis. Architecture at the end of the nineteenth century was in danger of being left behind by technological progress: by mechanization; by steel, glass and concrete. Academically educated architects clung to old architectural styles, not knowing how to respond to the new conditions that were replacing stone and brick.

The forms that opened the way for future developments were created more by engineers with no formal education in architecture than architects proper. Prominent examples are Joseph Paxton's Crystal Palace (1851) and Gustave Eiffel's Eiffel Tower (1889). The architectural world in the nineteenth century was in fact deeply split: on the one side, architects clinging to the tradition of past styles, and on the other side engineers who had started to use new materials outside architectural conventions. There was a rift that seemed impossible to bridge between art and technology.

Architecture as art was on the verge of extinction. If architecture lost all style and modality and all form was derived from calculation, then it would cease to be art.

Art Nouveau utilized steel's pliability to elaborate new possibilities for its usage. Moreover, in the design for the Paris Metro, the modern system of mass-producing the same object was also considered. In *Das Passagenwerk* (translated in English as *The Arcades Project*[5]) Walter Benjamin describes Art Nouveau as 'the last attempt at a sortie on the part of art imprisoned by technical advance within her tower.' In other words, Art Nouveau aimed to revive artistic architecture by introducing the possibilities of new technologies. Isn't this picture applicable to the conditions of 100 years later as well?

In the 1980s, postmodern architecture became the fashion and allusions to past styles were rampant. But Ito refused historic design and focused on plant-like elements, just as Gaudi and Art Nouveau referred to plants to become free of the rigidly styled architecture of the nineteenth century. At the end of the twentieth century, the architectural world experienced the wave of IT innovations, and due to dramatic developments in digital technology the concept of space itself was severely altered. This gave rise to outrageous arguments suggesting that the physical designing of architecture would become redundant if all space were to become information terminals. Then Sendai Mediatheque generated a universe of new geometry – just like a Big Bang in the architectural world.

Let us position the Mediatheque also in terms of the genealogy of Ito's works. In the 1970s, Ito worked on housing projects such as the White U house (1976) that were characteristically closed to the outside world. In the 1980s, however, he began to open his architecture to the city; this can be observed in Silver Hut (1984). He began to concern himself with designing membranes, with points of contact between building and environment. The Tower of Winds (1986) reflected the invisible flows in the surrounding environment. In the Yatsushiro Municipal Museum (1991) he succeeded in making a large volume appear light by integrating the architecture with landscape characterized by a mound on the front elevation. He was realizing a sense of lightness on both the scale of housing and of public facilities. In the 1990s, after this project, the focus of his work shifted to public facilities, and numerous projects were carried out throughout Japan.

Despite the fact that Ito's style is changing, the Sendai Mediatheque interestingly shares some characteristics with his first works. His early work, Aluminium House (1971), has a vertical cylinder at the centre which was conceived by Ito not only as a light well but also as an information terminal. In other words, the cylinder in the Aluminium House prefigured the tubes in the Sendai Mediatheque. It is notable that there is a vertical, and not just a horizontal, transparency in his architecture. Moreover, already in the House in Kasama (1981) Ito had dismantled hierarchy to pursue a flat space where fragments of forms floated around in the space.

After the Sendai Mediatheque The Sendai Mediatheque embodies the image of the information era. Despite this, its architecture is extremely architectural. In other words, the image of information was not expressed by abandoning architecture but by insisting on the application of architectural method. Or to put it in another way, Ito eliminated conventional 'architecture' by using an architectural method. In a situation where an element external to architecture, namely information technology, was threatening the existence of architecture, Ito dares to unite them. Behind the mask of information technology lies the concept of the duplex body. Ito believes that we possess one body as lived experience, and another body which tries to burst through it.

A body augmented by digital communication is different from the modern body. According to Ito, the floating body of electronic media requires a space that is not bound to a place. In the 1960s McLuhan argued that clothing and shelter are an extension of our skin. Similarly, Ito asserts that architecture should be a media-suit possessing a soft and fluid membrane: 'architecture is extended clothing, extended media-suit … people who wrap themselves up in media-suits, live in virtual nature, in the forest of media. They are tarzans in the forest of media.'[6] This is architecture for digital nomads.

Already in 1985 Ito had presented the idea of dwelling based in a fluffy tent with a bed and few pieces of furniture in the installation 'Pao for the Tokyo Nomad Girl'. It was not architecture of a potent male body, such as the Doric order in classical architecture or the architecture of Le Corbusier. It was not massive either. It was architecture as the body of a frivolous girl who daily goes to the convenience store. It was also different from modern architecture conceived as a device for achieving a healthy body. The new body is fluidity. It is interesting to note that the body-image of Art Nouveau also was soft and feminine, conjuring images of nature and of organic matter dissolving. The two may share the same images because of the emergence of an 'information' environment as a new 'nature'.

Ito's thinking did not stop here. It is still developing. This is what is truly startling when one considers his activities after the Sendai Mediatheque. In a lecture Ito gave at the symposium 'Alternative Modern', organized by me in 2004, he focused on the change in the concepts of function, abstraction, production and time, and on electronic function, self-generating geometry, agricultural production and non-linear process as the principles for a new architecture. In his attitude in constructing such statements, one senses his strong will to go beyond the modernism of which he is a legitimate inheritor. The keywords he mentioned perhaps pertained more to the territory which exists between the natural and the artificial rather than to the architectural. Most memorable of all was the impression I received of Ito as someone who was liberated from conventions, who had attained enlightenment. Collaboration with structural engineers, free sculptural creation, a keen sense of colour and organic spaces that arouse bodily sensations. Ito appeared as an architect who willingly plunged himself into change through interaction with others.

'Alternative modern' is my own neologism. It is based on the supposition that a different modernism is now emerging. If the postmodern was a rhetorical manipulation of existing architecture, then alternative modern is the liberation of the possibilities of a modernism which encompassed diverse directions such as Art Nouveau and Expressionism, but which subsequently contracted to form the international style. Ito is probably at the centre of this liberation. He presents a new geometry which generates complex spaces through simple rules, as well as new ornamentation that at times functions as a structural element. In Japan, his office is producing the greatest number of promising next-generation architects, such as Kazuyo Seijima, and is forming a network of architects as rich as that of Kenzo Tange's and Kiyonori Kikutake's offices in which Ito himself once worked.

Entering the twenty-first century, Ito's activities expanded into Spain, Belgium, England, France, Singapore, Taiwan and the United States, amongst other places. It would not be surprising if after the completion of a work of the calibre of the Sendai Mediatheque an architect found it difficult to take the next step, but Ito astoundingly continues to cross new frontiers: the Serpentine Gallery Pavilion (2002), where the pattern of the openings is defined by the trajectory of a unicursal line; the plan for the Pavilion in the Santa Cruz Garden and Park in Coimbra, reminiscent of a mesh of plants; the TOD'S Omotesando Building (2004), enveloped in a tree-like concrete structure; 'GRIN GRIN' (2005) in Fukuoka Island City Central Park, where the landscape becomes distorted; and the Taichung Metropolitan Opera House, which evokes images of the organs of living things. Presented with this outpouring of ideas at the cutting-edge of contemporary architecture, one is bound to question whether Ito may be supernaturally inspired.

The Tama Art University Library (2007) sees the heavy usage of the arch, an element which contemporary architecture has retreated from. But this is not a simplistic return to the past. The design with arches of disparate sizes would not be conceivable in the conventions of classical architecture. It is also different from the sensations conveyed by Expressionism. A luminous cave-like space spreads out on a skewed plane. The floor on the ground level is gently inclined to echo the site with its numerous sloping roads. The building stimulates us from the soles of our feet by internally introducing a design approximating the natural topography of the site. In his exhibition 'The New "Real" in Architecture' (2006), Ito also attempted a redesign of the floor surface akin to landscaping in order to address bodily sensations without confining himself to the displaying of models and drawings.

The exhibition was not a retrospective one. It focused on recent projects that came after the Sendai Mediatheque

and in which bold structural experiments were attempted. In other words, it was a display of Ito's present fierce momentum in creating unprecedented architecture. When I hosted a symposium held in conjunction with 'The New "Real"' in 2007, it seemed to me, listening to Ito's lecture, that the speed of his evolution had increased, as if time progresses at a different rate for him. There is no time for reiteration: continue to change further. This is a troublesome state of affairs for a critic. Any text written about him is bound to be left behind by the new real to which Ito would have by then already made a transition. The aforementioned body image of Ito, too, has probably shifted to one that rejoices in materials, one that is full of the energy of life.

By now, the Sendai Mediatheque seems to have happened a long, long time ago.

1   Noriko Takiguchi, *Nihon no Kenchikuka: Ito Toyo, Kansatsuki [Toyo Ito: Architect, Japan]* (Tokyo 2006)
2   Toyo Ito Interview, *Detail* (Japan), 2005/07
3   Toyo Ito, 'There is No New Architecture Without Being Immersed in the Sea of Consumption', Toyo Ito et al., *Toyo Ito: Blurring Architecture 1971–2005* (New York 1999)
4   Toyo Ito, 'The Transparent Urban Forest', Toyo Ito et al., *Blurring Architecture*
5   Walter Benjamin, *The Arcades Project*, ed. R. Tiedemann, tr. H. Eiland and K. McLaughlin (Cambridge, MA 2002)
6   Toyo Ito, 'Tarzans in the Forest of Media', Toyo Ito et al., *Blurring Architecture*

The Discovery of Process

RIKEN YAMAMOTO

House in White   I went to see Kazuo Shinohara's 'House in White' after hearing about its imminent dismantling and reconstruction in a different location. It was completed in 1966, so it is a work from more than 40 years ago. Because all furnishings and lighting fixtures were removed in preparation for the demolition, the space felt as empty as a cave. At the centre of this space, a single post of Japanese cedar stood not too far from a pure white wall. The ceiling was high. The white wall reached this high ceiling: it was enormous. The wall had one small door and an even smaller window diagonally above it. The space gave the impression that a dimensional alteration of only a few millimetres would wreck the whole design. It had been thought through to the most minute details. The fact that it had been thought through was quite apparent. Although I was familiar with photographic images of it, that was my first actual experience of the space. In fact I had not been particularly attracted to the work. I felt compelled to visit it before its demolition only because I knew that Toyo Ito had praised it as a stunning work.

Seeing the immense white wall and the cylindrical column that stands rather symbolically not too far from it, I instantly understood what had so stimulated and inspired Ito. I understood the reason why the sensibilities of this young architect who had only just begun to design architecture had been excited. The Ito of the time and the Ito of today overlapped and came together in my mind's eye as I stood in that hollow space.

What Ito had seen was a space of exceptional autonomy, one that seemed a pure product of Shinohara's imagination. By an exceptionally autonomous space, I mean the space had been formed with no relationship to various external factors, that is, conditions that offer constraints such as social, environmental and economic factors and consideration of everyday life. The House in White appeared to me to be fashioned solely out of an idea or thought that had formed inside Shinohara's mind. It was in this sense that the work was pure: it spurned any relationship with the external world. It was this purity that had attracted Ito to the work. To Ito's eyes, the space, which ignored all external factors and was formed solely as an extension of Shinohara's mind, must have appeared extraordinarily rational. I could feel the same intense attraction even though 40 years had passed since then. I share Ito's fascination with the purity of this work.

At the time, 40 years ago, architecture was something intended for everyday life. The issues that concerned architecture were issues that concerned the city. Architecture was all about its relationship to everyday life, or its relationship to the city. Whatever might be one's assessment of the conditions of everyday life and the urban environment, that is, however positive or negative they might seem, they were unavoidable external factors for architecture. Architecture was in fact created out of its relationship to those external factors. That was the prevailing idea at the time. The question of the 'purity of space' raised by Shinohara's philosophy, however, fundamentally challenged that idea, and seemed to open up new possibilities for architecture. It was this aspect of Shinohara's purity that resonated intensely with Ito.

I believe that throughout his career as an architect, his approach has been characterized by an ineluctable desire for purity of space:

'I believe that in the design process one should concentrate as much as possible on one's own ideas and present a model that has no relation to the demands of the client.'

'Presently, the only possible course of action open to me is to bear witness with a sense of regret to the distortion of my initial scheme by the client's desire for a home that conforms to the set of domestic skills he has mastered, budget restrictions or social factors such as building regulations, technological factors or factors related to human relationships, and after completion, the various additional demands of everyday life made by occupants.'

'To design is to track the progressive distortion of one's own intellectual process.'[1]

These are excerpts taken from a text written by Ito in 1971. He was 30 years old. Ito's strong belief in 'purity of space' is evident. He believed that space, which should fundamentally be pure, is distorted by external factors. By excluding all external factors, the space is made highly personal, and it is this personal quality that enables the space to be pure.

Kikutake and   Having graduated from university,
Shinohara   Ito started working at Kiyonori Kikutake's firm. Kikutake is well known as a member of the Metabolist movement, a group of architects that explored the nature of the rapidly changing city and the role of architecture in relation to that changing city; i.e. a group that asked basic questions concerning the relationship between the city and architecture. Kikutake is commonly regarded as a particularly logical architect who strove to reconstruct a new relationship between urban environment and architecture. The man himself, however, could not be more different from this reputation. 'His sketches, though fragmentary, were inspired and taught us young architects new possibilities of architecture and the joy of designs based on human sensitivity.'[2] Ito regarded Kikutake as an architect characterized not by logic but rather by an acute sensitivity that engendered a constant out-pouring of images. It has been said that his fierce and

complete faith in his own sensibility was akin to madness. 'I don't think there is any other architect for whom the expression "mad" is so applicable', wrote Ito.[3] Ito had a high regard for this internal madness, and was acutely critical of Kikutake's later endeavours at focusing more on the importance of the relationship with society and at becoming more socially involved. Ito was of the opinion that an architect should be strictly faithful to his own internal imagination and that, above all, the purity of those imaginings should be defended and maintained. Kikutake thought differently. His concern was that an insistence on purity might make architecture inaccessible to the outside world, make it lose its social dimension completely. 'Architectural creation has to acknowledge the contradictions of society, the contradictions of human beings. It is because of this that architecture strives to create order, strives to overcome contradictions.'[4] Architecture should be created with the assumption that it is to be created within society, being influenced and influencing that society; that was architecture as conceived by Kikutake.

Ito's view was the complete opposite. If by opening up to society the purity of one's imagination is lost, then it is better not to do so. Should we not choose madness instead of becoming a mediocre, socially engaged architect? This was the question that Ito posed Kikutake. It was also at the same time a fundamental question that he directed at himself.

For Ito, problems regarding the relationship between the purity of one's own idea and the various external factors that distort such purity, and the relationship architecture should have with its urban and social environment, were deeply felt. Shinohara's call for an architecture that is individual rather than social therefore made a more powerful impression on Ito than Kikutake's statement.

Shinohara was unequivocal in stating that regardless of how a city may be conceived, or what its conditions may be, houses designed by him were 'never created by conforming to them or by being inspired by them'.[5] Architecture should be conceived from the theories and ideas of individuals. Ito compares Shinohara's attitude with Kikutake's socially engaged approach and concludes that purity should be valued even if it means loss of engagement with society: 'My position is clearly the same as Shinohara's. Indeed, I am rather puzzled that architects working in the 1960s (like Kikutake) could so easily be convinced about the possibility of engagement with the city.'[6]

Exclusion of the External

Ito's architectural works at the time were even purer as spaces than Shinohara's. That is, they were extremely personal. The White U in Nakano is simply a pure white, hollow ring. Light enters this ring, making shadows move. The work is a white ring created solely for this interplay of light and shadow. It epitomizes Ito's belief in the purity of space. This house shuts out the outside world. It is a totally enclosed ring that has no relationship to the

Interior of Shinohara's House in White, Tokyo (1966)

surrounding urban spaces. The critic Koji Taki described its space as 'white darkness'.[7] The space, by its complete isolation from the outside world, certainly suggests a kind of darkness. The 'white darkness' itself ends up surrounding and forming a courtyard that resembles a basement dry area. In fact, this work would be just as effective had it been sunk below ground, so closed is it to the outside world. It is a work that is made up almost entirely of internal spaces. In other words, the outside world has been excluded.

However, the outside world has not been excluded in just a physical sense. The mode of thought behind the work is also closed. That is, the ideas of all others must be excluded as much as possible if one is to create a work that is faithful to one's own idea. The originality of one's idea cannot otherwise be guaranteed. That is what he means by his statement, 'I believe that in the design process one should concentrate as much as possible on one's own ideas and present a model that has no relation to the demands of the client.' This mode of thought, which is to have space reflect one's own idea as purely as possible, excludes all external influences. A 'pure space' is a space based on that original idea. A direct relationship is established between the thought original to oneself and that space. Only by doing so can 'purity of space' be achieved.

The U-House in Nakano is closed to the outside world, but it is not just physically closed to its urban environment. Ito's mode of thought excludes thoroughly the influence of external ideas, that is, the ideas of others. The fact that the space is closed to the urban environment is only the inevitable consequence of that intellectual isolation.

In all likelihood, his experience with the U-House made him aware of such closure for the first time. The question of how this closure might be dissolved while 'purity of space' was assured subsequently became his greatest concern. Would not an approach based on social involvement such as

'Glass' model of Sendai

the one adopted by Kikutake, result in the loss of one's purity? Ultimately, is not a 'pure space' such as Shinohara's, which can only be achieved because it is personal, unable to break out of its closure? Those were the questions that Ito asked himself.

What to do then? Looking back on Ito's work, I feel that this fundamental question he asked himself – how was he to free himself from purity, that is, the spell of closure that purity cast? – has been the very essence of his architecture. Ito has continued to regard this as an issue that he must come to grips with, whatever the circumstances.

The Experience of the Sendai Mediatheque   Silver Hut, Tower of Winds in Yokohama, Yatsushiro Municipal Museum, T-Building in Nakameguro, Akahiko Memorial Museum, Odate Jukai Dome. All the works that were successively presented after the White U had as their underlying theme the question of how he might free himself from purity and the binding spell that purity effectively casts. All these works were critically acclaimed. However, I believe they did not fully satisfy Ito. The works all had clear messages addressed to the present age and to current circumstances. Questions raised by the present age and current circumstances were brilliantly answered. But were these messages not achieved through the loss, however slight, of that purity to which Ito aspires? Is it not true that the stronger the message for the present age and social environment, the greater the sacrifice of purity? That was precisely what Ito himself had criticized about Kikutake. These earlier works by Ito appear to me to be wavering between two poles: the pursuit of purity and the acknowledgement of external factors that distort such purity. Ito had not yet discovered a clear answer.

It was the experience of the Sendai Mediatheque that swept away all these vacillations. During the process from

initial conception to eventual realization, he was liberated for the first time from the spell of purity.

Ito once spoke to me about his idea for the Sendai Mediatheque competition. It was before his scheme was made public. Radiating a sense of accomplishment that was in marked contrast to his usual composure, he spoke to me with the enthusiasm of someone who has come up with a groundbreaking idea. 'If they don't accept my proposal …' he said, leaving the rest unspoken. It was easy to guess what he meant: if they don't accept my proposal, their qualification to judge is highly suspect. He seemed to have absolute certainty about his idea. I still clearly remember the way he talked, beaming with confidence. The model that I later saw was delicate and transparent; as Ito had said, it was unlike any building I had ever seen. It was neither a rigid-frame structure nor a load-bearing wall structure. Its floor slabs, supported by transparent shafts, would undoubtedly be used in a very different way from floors supported in a conventional manner by a grid of beams and columns. With a rigid-frame or load-bearing wall structure, the structural system determines the way floors are used. That is because the evenly distributed columns or walls give a certain order to the floor space. In other words, the architecture is designed so that from the start the structural system and the architectural programme are in accord. The Sendai Mediatheque was different. It was not premised on any programme, nor did it encourage the adoption of one. Put simply, it was not obvious from the floor plans how the building ought to be used. Ito's strong desire for a particular structural framework seemingly took precedence and was satisfied without regard for other factors. The scheme seems shaped, not by the programme or by demands made by society, the city or any other external factor, but by a pure, personal, formal concern on Ito's part. Would this really work as architecture? What most worried the competition judges must have been the question: 'is this architectural scheme realizable?' The scheme was such a radical departure from all known architectural typologies. It was a work totally preoccupied with spatial purity. That was precisely why the model was beautiful. The scheme made possible a model that looked just like a transparent glass sculpture.

If Ito had stubbornly tried to realize the model as it was, the architectural result would probably have been quite different. If Ito had resisted the distortion of this pure space by various external factors, then the building would have been significantly different from its present form. Perhaps an attempt could have been made to translate the transparent glass sculpture directly into architecture. Had that purity been achieved, however, it would no doubt have been distorted the moment the building began to be used.

However, Ito did not resist distortion. Instead of attempting to achieve the scheme in its pure form, he actively solicited and accepted many ideas from outside; that is, he willingly introduced different ways of thinking into that process. At the time this work was subjected to fairly fierce

criticism. The work was deemed too personal. Why was such a personal work going to be constructed on that spot as a public building? Is this building of unprecedented appearance truly public in character? That was the gist of the criticism. The majority of people, especially in Japan, still believe that a building that directly reflects the individuality of the architect cannot be public in character. They think an architect should listen to as many opinions as possible and create a standard building. Ito seems to have communicated with people holding such opinions as well.
I believe it was because Ito talked to them and listened to their views that those who initially opposed his scheme eventually accepted it. This process was an unexpected experience for Ito as well. It made him realize that external factors and opinions do not necessarily distort the purity of architecture and that, on the contrary, the external can endow a building with greater vitality. It was an experience that fundamentally changed his way of thinking.

Empathic Architecture In the process of realizing the Sendai Mediatheque, Ito's fundamental question – how can the pure space created within oneself be opened to the outside world – became a quite specific concern. The process of architectural realization is a process of studying construction methods and details and solving every conceivable aspect of building including mechanical systems such as air-conditioning and electrical wiring, as well as a process of empathy, that is, a process of getting others to empathize with images, ideas and inspirations that one has conceived inside oneself. The solution that Ito arrived at through experience was not to try to maintain his purity, but to re-examine from a different perspective the very idea that he himself was pure. By a different perspective, I mean a relativistic perspective. To adopt a relativistic perspective is to allow oneself to change in the process of architectural realization. Ito realized for the first time that discovering this changing self was a part of the architectural process. It was entirely different from his previous mode of thought, which was to see pure space being distorted by external factors.

There is no point in creating architecture if one loses the will to achieve a pure space, a space that is pure precisely because it is personal, even if it is madness. I believe Ito still holds firmly to that belief. The change wrought by his experience with the Sendai Mediatheque was a realization that this pure space is capable of changing through its relationship to the outside world. There is no method for opening up a pure space to the outside world while preserving its purity. To open up a space to the outside, that is, to gain the empathy of others, one must allow oneself to change in the process. Ito came to realize that change does not distort purity but instead enables him to achieve a richer architecture.

A pure space is something that is created within oneself and is therefore extremely personal. Is that not, however, a space so abstract it cannot even be considered architecture? The purity of a pure space is an abstract concept. Is not a pure space as illusory as the notion of being able to give material form to such a space while preserving its abstract character? Transforming a pure space into a building is probably impossible without acknowledging external factors. The discovery of the impossibility of 'pure space' – that was what Ito experienced in the Sendai Mediatheque.

There is something I realized in witnessing the struggle that Ito went through. Purity, that is, the spell of closure cast by purity, is in fact a contradiction inherent in modern architecture itself. The theory of modern architecture made it imperative for spaces to be pure. Though many of us may have realized that contradiction, it took a long struggle for us to find a way out of it. What Ito discovered in the process of realization was not a way of giving precedence to external factors that distort the purity of space, or a formalism that abandons any effort at opening up the space to the outside world, or a cynicism that allows him to pretend that he alone stands on the outside, but a way of transforming his own purity into an actual building. Through that process, Ito experienced the moment when abstract space becomes actual.

An actual building always exists in the context of external factors such as its place, its time, its history and its community. To become actual, an abstract space must come into contact with, and become closely related to, things such as a specific place, time and community culture. Let me repeat, this does not by any means signify the loss of purity of the space. It is on the contrary a process in which Ito's uniqueness and purity come to be accepted by people as a symbol of that place, that time, that history and that community.

1   Toyo Ito, *Shinkenchiku* (October 1971)
2   Toyo Ito, 'Kiyonori Kikutake: Teach Us How to Survive Our Madness', *Kenchiku Bunka* (July 1975)
3   Ibid
4   Kiyonori Kikutake, 'Contemporary Image of the Architect', *Kenchiku Bunka* (April 1965)
5   Shinohara, 'Theory of Houses', *Shinkenchiku* (April 1967)
6   Ito, 'Kiyonori Kikutake'
7   Koji Taki, 'The Concept of "Form"', *Shinkenchiku*, (November 1976)

CAVE HOUSES

Most of my early works from the 1970s on into the first part of the 1980s were virtually sealed in by white walls. My thinking was that by sealing off connexions with the external environment I might heighten the degree of abstraction and create more beautiful interiors by means of controlled natural light. Among these works, **White U** was the most radically self-contained. Visitors to the house often commented that it seemed just like an underground chamber. Indeed, apart from one large opening on to a courtyard, openings through the walls were few and small, the interior depending mainly upon sunlight from above, hence the subterranean feeling. The pure 'white tube' living space bends in one continuous linear motion around the courtyard, so that the family perpetually moved about the periphery. Moreover, the courtyard itself was contained by a concrete wall, so even in this central Tokyo location a strangely isolated stillness pervaded. In 1997, the family decided to have the house taken down. I designed **House in Kasama** for a ceramic artist couple who were taken with White U. But whereas White U was an uncompromising aesthetic exercise, Kasama being more consciously conceived as a dwelling, refined those aesthetics in a more rational manner. The facade in particular is markedly different. Kasama, built using 2×4 wood-frame construction, comprises two volumes under a gabled roof and pent roof respectively. The main volume dominated by a curved white wall could almost be a slice of White U, but the design of openings and the furnishings designed to harmonize with the grey-painted board walls are much more skilful. The gable-roofed volume serves both as an entrance hall and as a small gallery space for exhibiting ceramics.

Located in midtown Tokyo, White U lay in a residential area, and looked out on the Shinjuku skyscrapers nearby. The locality is a mixture of wooden houses, blocks of flats, and medium and small apartments.

A reinforced concrete structure of two walls enclosed a horseshoe-shaped central courtyard covering about 75 square metres. Between the walls there was an interior, ring-like space, covered by a roof slab which sloped towards the centre. The tubular interior extended around the building, and was finished in pure white, with daylight entering from above and from the sides. The gradation of the lighting gave a soft nuance to the space inside, marking a clear contrast with the courtyard, which was also encompassed by architectural concrete walls.

White U

TOKYO, JAPAN, 1976

△ View from the roof
◁ View of dining space from living space
→ Aerial view

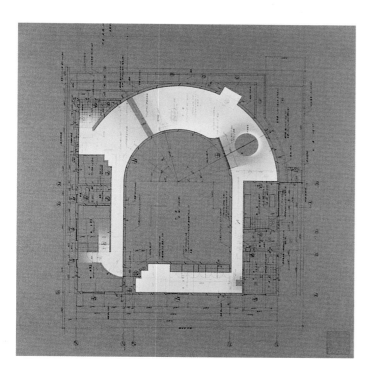

△ Floorplan
▷ Living space
← View toward courtyard from dining space

House in Kasama

KASAMA, JAPAN, 1981

This house covers 290 square metres and utilizes a 'two-by-four' wooden structural system. The T-shaped building slopes down towards the south, allowing the south wing to be two-storeyed, whereas the north side consists of only one level. The two ridges of the roof intersect to form the entrance to the house. All of the external walls are enclosed by a flexible waterproof covering.

The house was designed to respond to the requirements of the client, a ceramic artist. It is divided into three functional sections: a small gallery under the northern gabled roof, which connects to the entrance, a studio and bedroom in the basement area of the south ridge, and a living space on the upper floor.

The house marks a progression in design from the seventies to the eighties. It has an area enclosed by walls like the earlier project, White U, is centripetal, and possesses a serious atmosphere, characteristics that were common in the former era. However, the house indicates clearly how Ito's architecture advanced into the eighties with the development of an open plan and multi-centred spaces.

→ View of entrance
▽ View from north

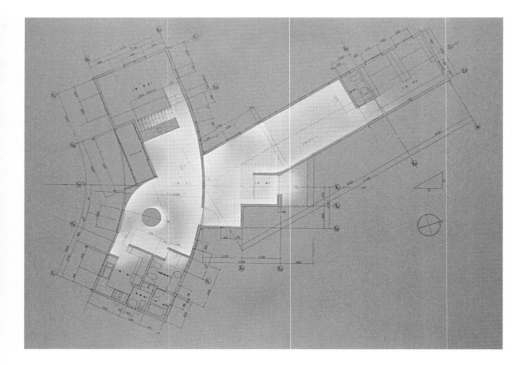

◁ Floorplan
▽ Living space
→ Gallery space

INCLUSIVE HOUSES

Almost in reaction to the 1970s, my works from this period are open and concrete, diametrically opposed to the abstract, closed spaces of my previous works. The predominant concrete walls give way to steel frames, making for a much lighter expression. **Silver Hut** was my own private residence, built on a lot immediately adjacent to the White U. The roof suggests a village of huts, vaults large and small perching on a series of steel trusses that span free-standing concrete columns. The 'Silver Hut' name alludes to an urban-primitive hut composed of aluminium and steel materials. Various minutely articulated rooms surround a central courtyard covered by a membrane-like metallic screen. Emblematic of the new household openly shared by all without the onerous, shut-in image of families past, everything looks and feels very light. Everything from the kitchen and furnishings to the doors and windows is metal-finished, smartly designed for a carefree, relaxed lifestyle. **House in Magomezawa** follows up on such Silver Hut concepts. The ground floor is a concrete-walled box atop which sits a con-trasting open volume framed in lightweight steel. The expanded aluminium mesh over the twin-vaulted roof and facade reinforce a very physical 'metallic hut' image. In retrospect, these residential projects can be seen as preliminary trials toward a series of late-1980s works that emphasize lightness and transparency.

Silver Hut

TOKYO, JAPAN, 1984

Silver Hut is just fifteen minutes by train from Shinjuku, and is located in a residential area in the centre of Tokyo. It is composed of a flat floor, concrete posts erected at 3.6 metre intervals, and a steel frame roof with seven shallow vaults positioned over the posts. The gable of the roof runs from north to south.

A courtyard covered by a portable tent is positioned in the centre of the south side of the house. This construction permits ventilation and sunshine to be easily controlled. The courtyard is an almost exterior space which can be used for a variety of functions, according to the season and the weather. Along the western side are the utility room, kitchen and a bedroom in the form of a concrete box half-buried below ground, and a child's room above on the mezzanine.

The north side accommodates the dining area and living room, while on the east there is a study and Japanese room, each covered by separate vaults; minimal walls, furniture or screens separate each room. The furniture is handmade or fashioned from old car parts: the fixtures found throughout emphasize practical functions.

△ View from south at night
▷ View of Japanese-style room

△ South view from courtyard
◁ View from south
→ Following page: Aerial view of Silver Hut and White U

North elevation

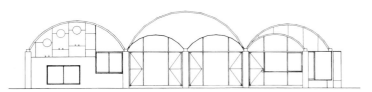

South elevation

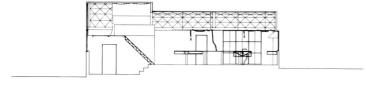

Cross section

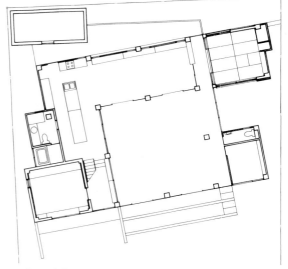

Ground-floor plan

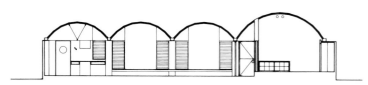

Longitudinal section

◄ View of kitchen
▷ Overall view
▽ View of courtyard

Magomezawa is a residential region close to Funabashi City that is approximately one hour by train from Tokyo. The house is constructed from reinforced concrete and steel. The ground floor utilizes a concrete wall formation, with an architectural concrete finish on both the interior and exterior.

Sunk just below ground level, the floor is finished with trowel-laid mortar, forming a concrete box enclosed by two steel frame vaults. Below the vaults there is a small bedroom, approximately 20 metres square, which is partitioned from the main space by sashes.

The construction allows light and wind to pass freely through the bedroom, in contrast to the kitchen and living room on the ground floor. These rooms are both enclosed by the concrete walls and are linked by a utility room and a terrace, but form two very different spaces.

Galvanized steel panels are used for the facade, forming skin-like membranes which let in daylight and fresh air. These panels are similar to those found on building sites to protect areas temporarily closed to the public.

House in Magomezawa

CHIBA, JAPAN, 1986

→ View from east
▽ View from east at night

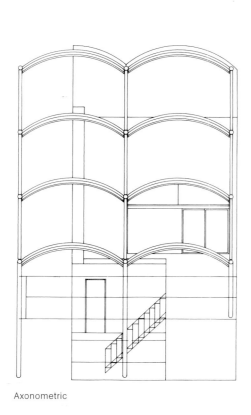

Axonometric

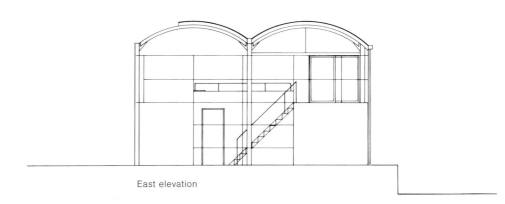

East elevation

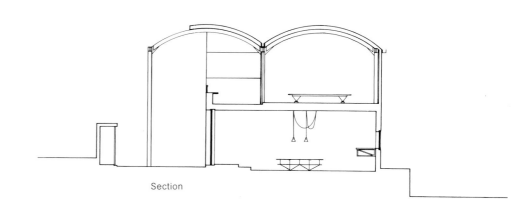

Section

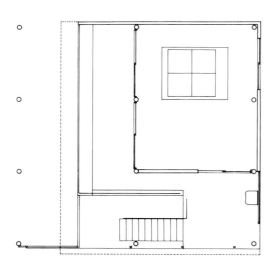

First-floor plan

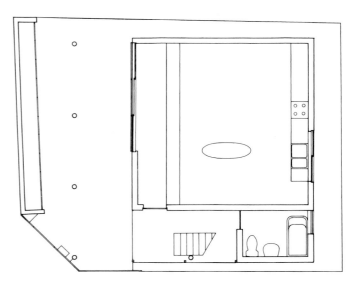

Ground-floor plan

△ Terrace on first floor
▷ Ground-floor interior

UNHEAVY
METAL

When Japan's 'bubble' economy peaked during the latter half of the 1980s, values were easily swayed by information that often had no actual basis. Especially in major cities like Tokyo, countless commercial buildings were constructed and destroyed in rapid succession. People wandered the streets in a stupor of consumption, enjoying the fleeting atmosphere. My installation Tokyo Nomad Girl's Yurt was intended to question the meaning of dwelling in a consumer city of the bubble years, drawing an analogy between the Mongolian nomad travelling about with a yurt as an extended 'wearable' and the urbanite revelling in the rootless consumer life. The three works in this section all depict images of architecture in an ethereal climate. The **Tower of Winds in Yokohama** project, for instance, was a commission to refurbish a ventilation tower over an underground shopping centre at Yokohama station. Merely a cylindrical structure sheathed in aluminium panels by day, at evening it loses its physicality and becomes a folly of myriad lights, perhaps modelled on the flamboyance and ephemerality of the city of the times. **Egg of Winds** was likewise a commission for a housing estate gate, with largely the same concept. **Restaurant Bar 'Nomad'**, designed from the very outset as a temporary structure in the nightclub district of Roppongi, was demolished after only two and a half years. Similar to a steel-framed circus tent in construction, the interior evanesced with shiny perforated aluminium panels, expanded alloy mesh strips and translucent fabrics suspended from the ceiling. Customers felt as if they were dining at an open-air foodstall and the place thronged night after night with hedonistic nomads. Surely no building so physically and psychologically embodied the notion of 'ephemerality'.

Tower of Winds in Yokohama

KANAGAWA, JAPAN, 1986

◁ Night view
▽ View of aluminium panels from interior
→ 1,280 mini-bulbs are arranged in a grid pattern

In the centre of a roundabout near Yokohama train station, a 21-metre tall tower was constructed covered in synthetic mirrored plates and encased in an oval aluminum cylinder. Floodlights positioned within these two layers, when lit, give the tower the appearance of a giant kaleidoscope.

The reflective properties of the aluminium panels emphasize the tower's simple metallic form during the day. At night the 'kaleidoscope' is illuminated, presenting a brilliant display of reflection upon reflection.

The tower consists of 1,280 small lights and 12 bright-white, vertically arranged neon light rings. Computer-controlled floodlights (30 in total, 24 on the interior, the remainder on the exterior) make patterns of light within the tower, according to the time of day.

Natural elements such as environmental noises and the speed and direction of the wind, affect the intensity of the floodlights, resulting in a controlled 'natural' phenomenon. The panels sometimes become a translucent film, at other times they appear to rise floodlit to the tower's surface.

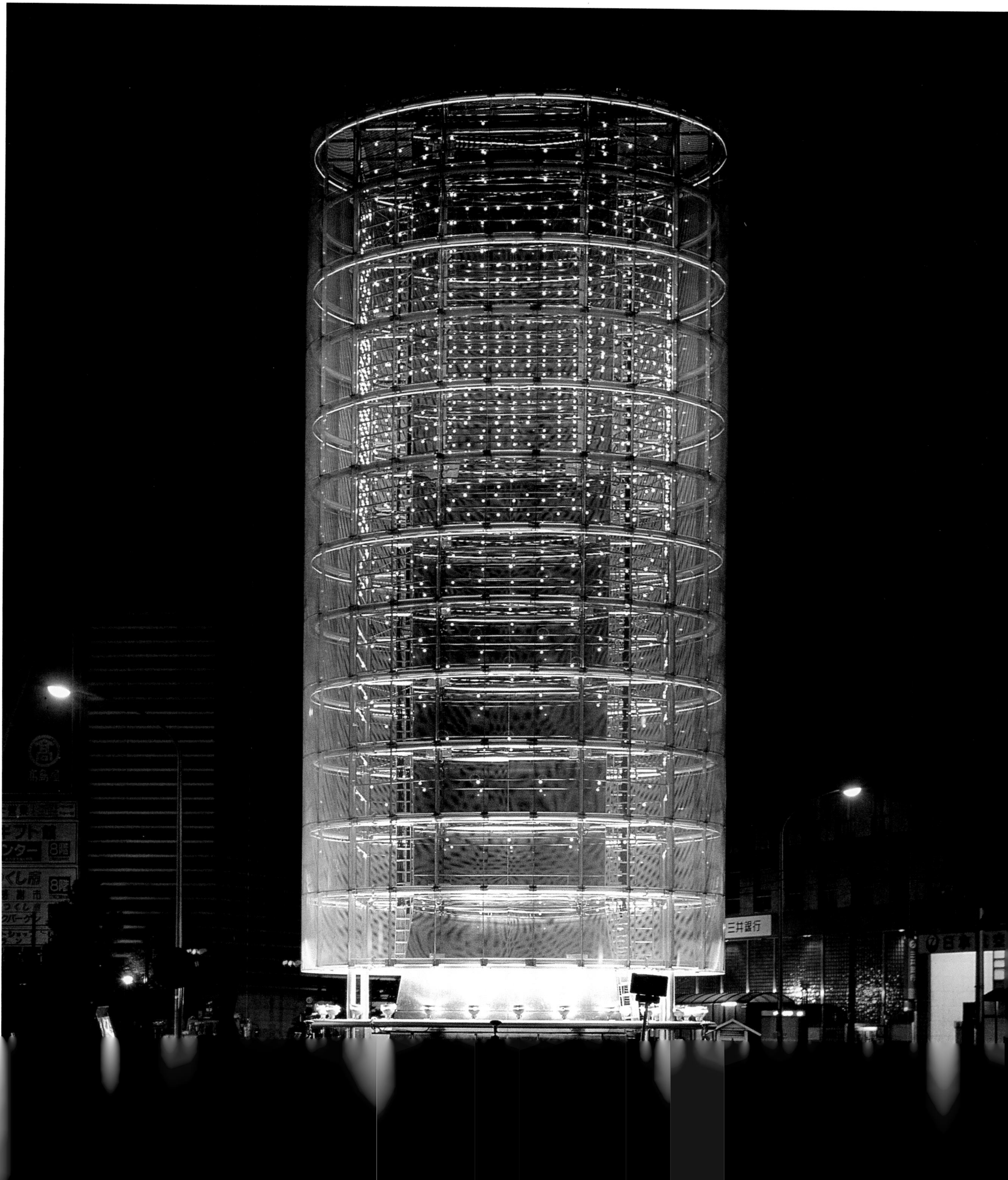
三井銀行

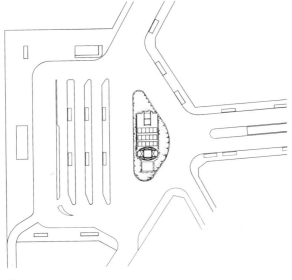

Site plan

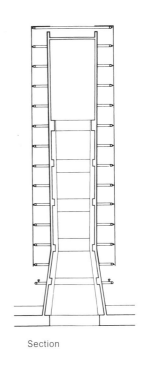

Section

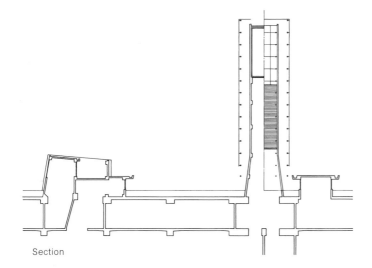

Section

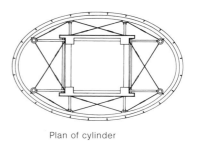

Plan of cylinder

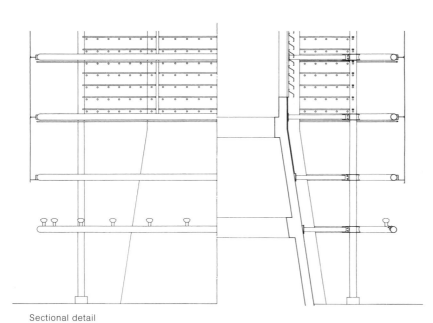

Sectional detail

→ 12 white neon rings in cylinder

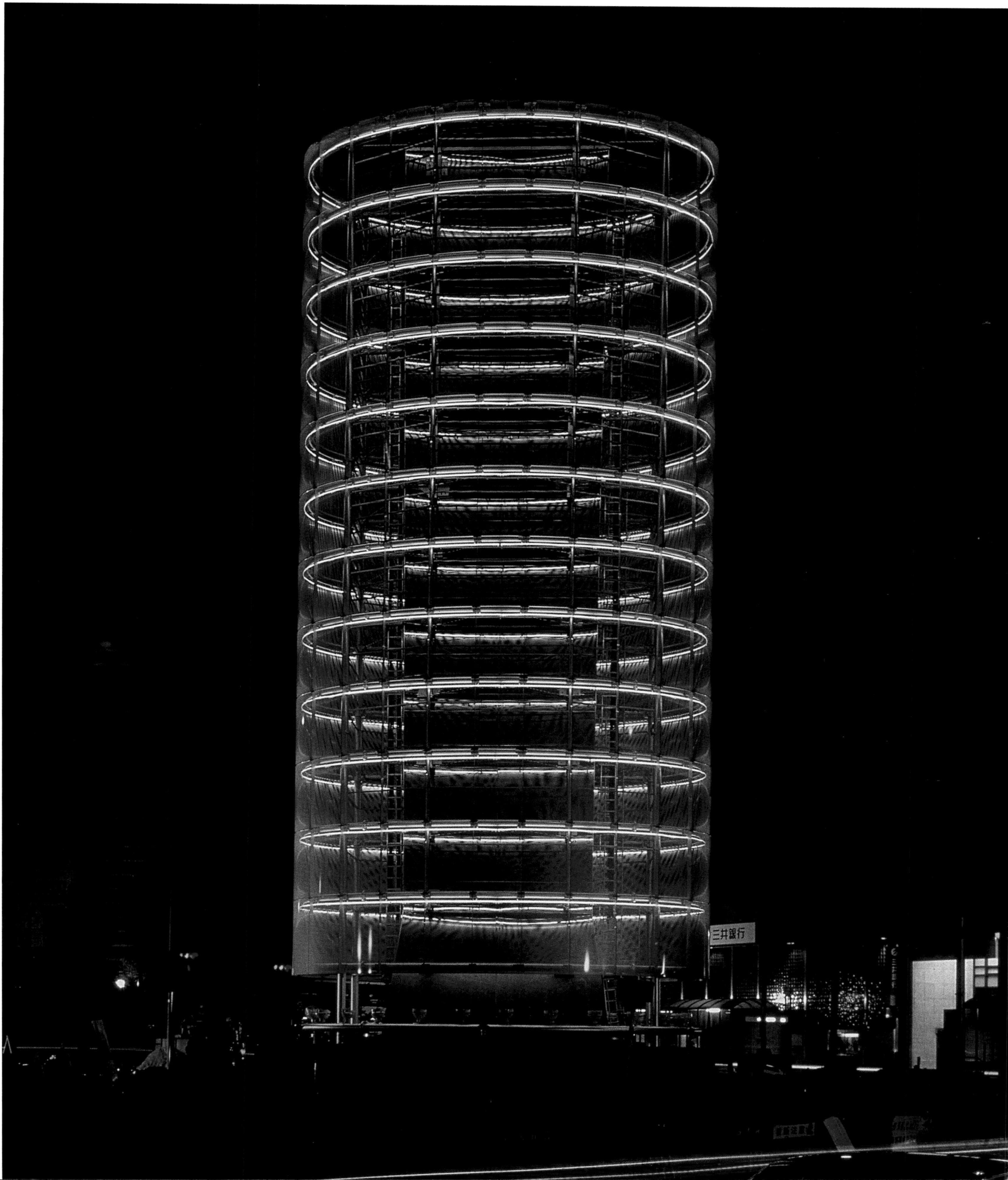
三井銀行

This rotating oval 'egg' 16 metres wide and 8 metres deep, floats 4 metres above ground on top of the entrance to a car park belonging to the Okawabata River City 21 residential complex. Encased in 188 panels, 60 of which are perforated aluminium, it looks matt silver during the day. In the evening dusk, as people come home from work, the built-in projection unit and lighting system start to operate, silently transforming the Egg of Winds into a visual display unit.

Five liquid-crystal projectors implanted within the egg project images on to two rear screens and on to the faces of the perforated panels. The projected picture is computer controlled, utilizing three kinds of lighting equipment and five image sources.

The projected source of lighting enables the Egg of Winds to present a new form of spatial advertising through information and images, where video artists may exhibit their work and information for residents can be aired.

Egg of Winds

TOKYO, JAPAN, 1991

→ Projection on Egg of Winds
▽ General view

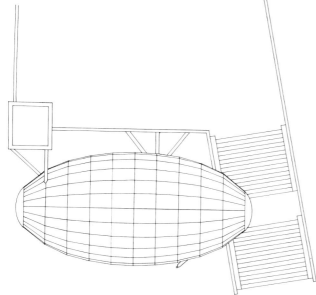

Roof plan

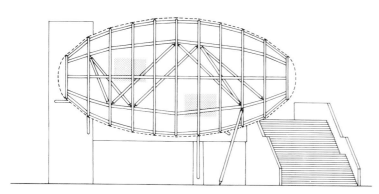

Section

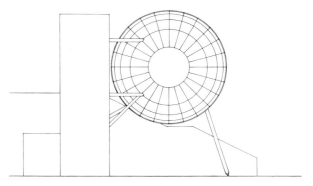

Elevation

Designed as a temporary structure to bypass a planning delay, the Nomad restaurant and bar lay in Tokyo's popular social district, Roppongi.

The atmosphere inside recalled a theatre: everything looked staged, from the entrance hall, fixtures and menu, to the waiters' clothes and background music. The simple event of eating a meal and chatting with friends was transformed into a fictional and surreal affair.

Taking on the form of an enormous tent, the Nomad was an oasis for travellers in the urban 'desert' of Tokyo, and for those who lived life on a whim. Visitors were drawn in by the bright neon lights of the restaurant.

A steel-frame construction ensured that the permitted building volume and height were maximized within planning regulations and expenditure restraints. The main construction materials, fabric and perforated aluminium, floated within this frame, creating the tent-like environment; resolutely, there was no architectural form, the tentlike building defied a consistent, determined design. The interior setting was filtered by a diffuse layer of finishes and furniture, effecting an illusory architectural quality. The diners appeared to become nomads, seated at tables beneath metallic clouds fluttering in the artificial breeze.

Restaurant Bar 'Nomad'

TOKYO, JAPAN, 1986

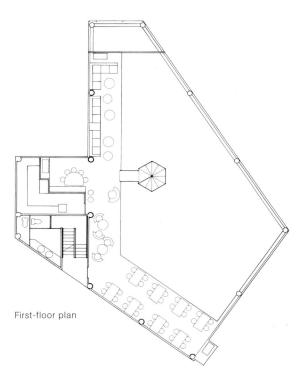

First-floor plan

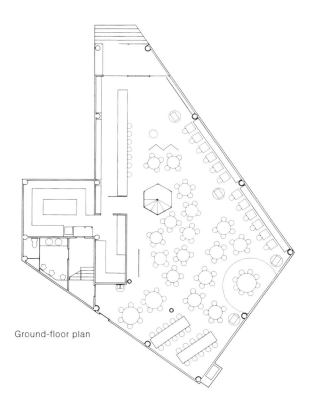

Ground-floor plan

◁ Temporary Noh stage
→ Interior view
→ View of entrance
→ Following pages: View upward

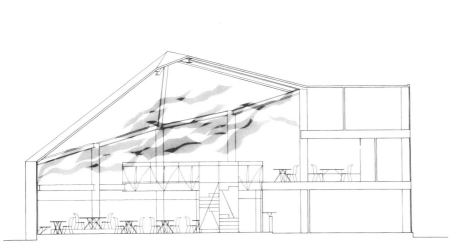

Section

TRANSPARENT WALLS

Up to this point, I had never used glass in a major way, perhaps because I'd always felt glass to be more of a barrier between interior and exterior than even walls. I preferred *shoji*, the papered sliding doors used in traditional Japanese architecture, as a gentler if less transparent means of partitioning spaces inside and out. It's also why I often utilize perforated aluminium sheets or expanded mesh on facades. Then for the first time in 1990, I included a glass facade in my proposal for the Maison de la culture du Japon à Paris design competition. A liquid-crystal film sandwiched between layers of glass could switch electrically from transparent to semi-opaque, thereby changing the whole look of the building. Inside this 'Mediatheque on the Seine' floated three spaceship-like 'media ships' that would alternately be seen through the facade or hidden behind overlapping reflections of the river front, something altogether new and different. Although we lost the competition, I continued to develop this glass facade idea elsewhere in the 1990s. Two smaller office buildings in this section, the **ITM Building in Matsuyama** and the **T Building in Nakameguro** also feature translucent glass facades, which conduct soft, natural daylight into light-wells whose stairways, lifts, plumbing and air-conditioning ducts are all exposed in their full metallic detailing. These light-wells with their vertical flow lines create visual relationships between levels and greatly improve communications throughout, which in turn later inspired the tube structures of the Sendai Mediatheque. One might say I was striving to shape a model of the dedicated small office building within the urban disorder of Tokyo.

This building houses the head offices of the associated companies of the long-established confectioner Ichiroku. The site is in a residential district on the southern border of Matsuyama.

The building, which is dedicated to office space like the Nakameguro T Building (1990), is classified in the Japanese Building Standards Act as an intermediate structure: in-between the highest level of fire resistance and the common wooden building. It has a three-level void space on the 1,500 square metre site containing stairways, small kitchen areas, toilets and other open-plan functions. The space of the void is animated by the presence of people and objects. It constitutes a new kind of 'communication location' where the people working can meet and chat in a relaxed environment. Offices are dispersed around the core, which houses the ground-floor rectangular entrance hall, and the first-floor break rooms.

Daylight is introduced from different directions into each individual functional area, and the result is a building filled with light. In the three-level void space a huge glass screen is integrated with the structural column system. The glass screen is covered with a milky translucent film, which blocks ultraviolet light and softens the intensity of the afternoon sun. During the day, light for the offices filters through the multifaceted aluminium curtain wall shaped to fit the site.

Skylights are provided in the break rooms, allowing light to pass through the glass floor to the entrance hall beneath. The ITM is an open-plan building with very few walls dividing the spaces. For this reason, indirect light provided to individual areas disperses, giving the interior of the building a homogeneous quality. Moreover, this light reflects off the aluminium, glass, white ceramic tile and other surfaces, breaking with the fixed conceptions of floor, wall and ceiling. The subdued light diffused by these surfaces disturbs perceptions of direction: the interior of the building is suffused with a weightlessness and the feeling of floating.

ITM Building in Matsuyama
EHIME, JAPAN, 1993

▷ Entrance hall
→ Main stair

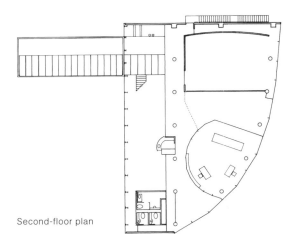

Second-floor plan

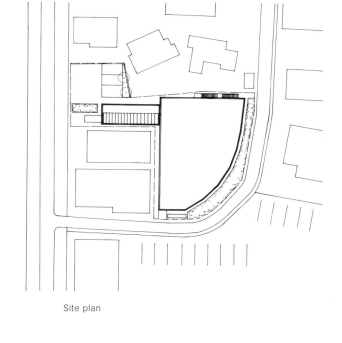

Site plan

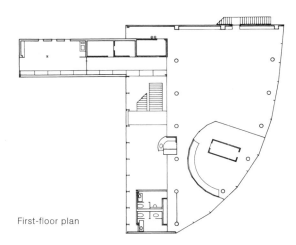

First-floor plan

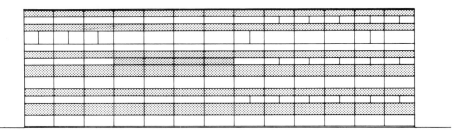

South elevation

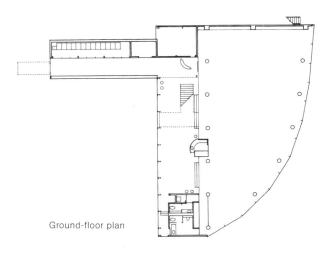

Ground-floor plan

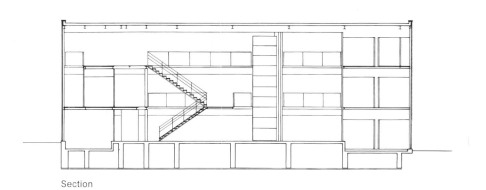

Section

△ South facade
▷ Detail of south facade

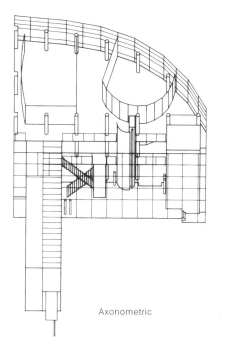

Axonometric

74

T Building in Nakameguro

TOKYO, JAPAN, 1990

This project is situated at the intersection of commercial, industrial and residential areas, and is bordered by both tall buildings and family housing.

Along the boundary with the street, a 'skin' made from a translucent film is attached to a long screen. The areas designated for office space are combined into one location, such that they can easily adapt to various purposes as necessary. Between this area and the screen is a three-storey void, which contains 'hovering' services (lavatory booths, stairs, deck slabs and a glazed steel lift shaft) that are all suspended from the ceiling.

People only remain in this transitory space for short periods, giving it an atmosphere of constant flux. The screen blurs the concept of inside and outside; one permeates the other. At times this void seems to be an assimilated part of the building; at others it appears completely separate. It illustrates the illusion of 'reality', in much the same way that an aquarium provides a 'natural' environment.

This building harmonizes the perceptions of architecture and landscape. The light nature of the structure reveals an evanescence amidst the constant fluidity and chaos of the city.

△ Toyo Ito with office staff
▷ View toward street from entrance lobby
→ Exterior facade

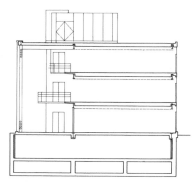

Section

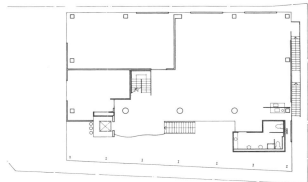

Second-floor plan

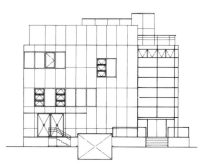

Northeast elevation

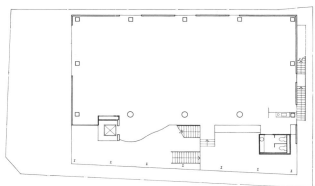

First-floor plan

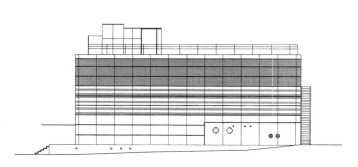

Northwest elevation

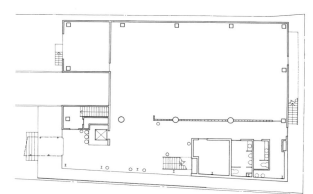

Ground-floor plan

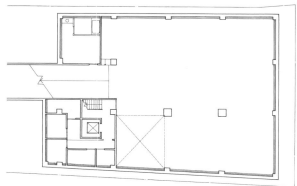

Basement floor plan

△ View upward toward the office area from entrance lobby
◁ Staircase in entrance lobby

MUSEUMS

We started designing what was to be our first public work, the **Yatsushiro Municipal Museum**, in 1988 when I was already 47. In Japan, younger architects rarely get a chance to take on public projects, nor can one easily enter competitions without a track record of achievements. Within these circumstances, our lucky break came via Kumamoto Art Polis, an independent regional scheme launched by Kumamoto Prefecture on the south-western island of Kyushu to select architects for their public projects. The prefectural authorities appointed a commissioner (Arata Isozaki; I have since inherited the position), who then suggested candidate architects for particular projects. The scheme is still active after two decades. The design for the museum further developed themes of lightness and buoyancy seen in the Silver Hut and other works of the 1980s. Here the volume above ground is largely concealed behind a grassy mound, so the roof arcs seem to float over the lawn, an expression of lightness I had thought would open new frontiers in public architecture. Sadly, I was not able to advance new programme proposals for the museum exhibits, which focused on local history and ethnology. The **Shimosuwa Municipal Museum** is another case in point: however innovative the architectural expression, the exhibition programme itself remained wholly status quo. Nonetheless, these two experiences with public architecture incited me to push the envelope even further thereafter; the lesson being that unless new designs spring from proposals for fresh approaches to actual use there can never be truly appealing public buildings. Designed around the same time as Yatsushiro, the **Gallery U in Yugawara** is a small private art space located next door to the client's weekend home. Once again we utilized the exact same structural system as in Yatsushiro: a thin roof vault over a series of small steel trusses.

Yatsushiro Municipal Museum was one of the first major projects for the Art Polis programme organized by the Kumamoto Prefecture. The programme, which was the idea of Kumamoto Prefecture and Arata Isozaki, aimed to coordinate the work of architects in order to make the Prefecture a cultural and architectural centre. As a result, the city of Yatsushiro wished to build a new museum to house under one roof its many historical artefacts, which were previously stored in several different locations, and contribute to establishing Yatsushiro as a cultural centre in Kyushu.

The museum is situated in a historical area near the old moat of the now dilapidated Yatsushiro castle. Opposite is Shohinken, an Edo period villa of the Matsui family who governed the area at that time. The first impressions of the site are the low, horizontal profile of Shohinken and the flatness of the leafy site itself.

This, added to the request that as many as possible of the existing trees be preserved, gave rise to the idea of the new museum as a park. Reducing the building volume and maintaining a park-like atmosphere seemed the most appropriate response to a site of this nature. A major problem was that the museum criteria and the ratio of building to site area required at least three storeys.

Efforts were concentrated on achieving these criteria without completely overshadowing the villa. The main concern in the process of this design was to avoid the massiveness predominating the conventional museum and to create a more light and bright space.

Thus the largest space, which includes the main exhibition hall, was placed on the ground floor and covered by an artificial hill. Since the ground floor is submerged, the first floor appears to be at ground level. A curved ramp runs over the hill and alongside a wall, providing a feeling of continuity with the natural plane of the landscape. There is a scenic view over the hill down to the street. The third floor is a hovering cylinder above the multi-vaulted roof of the main building and houses the artefact storage. In contrast to conventional museums where storage is located out of sight, the aim was to show that a museum stores artefacts as well as exhibits them.

Different structural systems were used in response to the purpose of each space. The first floor has a low ceiling height to conserve space. A steel frame multi-vaulted roof covers the second floor to provide light. The rear of the building consists of a reinforced concrete frame structure. By combining these different structures and spaces, an attempt was made to create a museum where people can enjoy not only the artefacts, but also the building itself.

Yatsushiro Municipal Museum

KUMAMOTO, JAPAN, 1991

△ General view from southeast
▷ Aerial view
← Entrance lobby

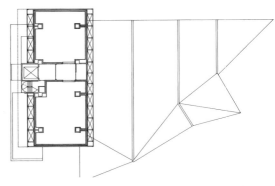

Third-floor plan

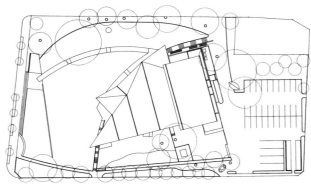

Site plan

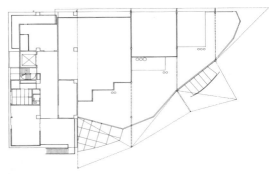

Second-floor plan

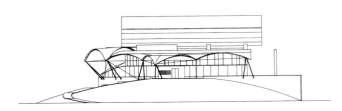

North elevation

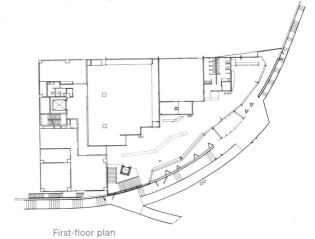

First-floor plan

East elevation

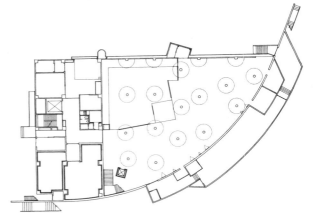

Ground-floor plan

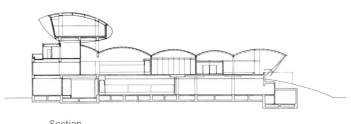

Section

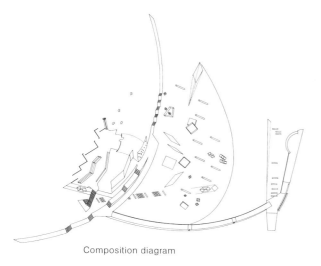

Composition diagram

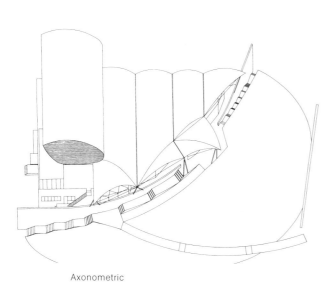

Axonometric

△ Café area
◁ View from east

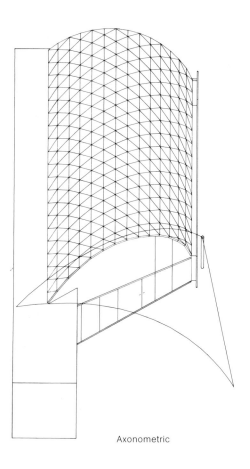

Axonometric

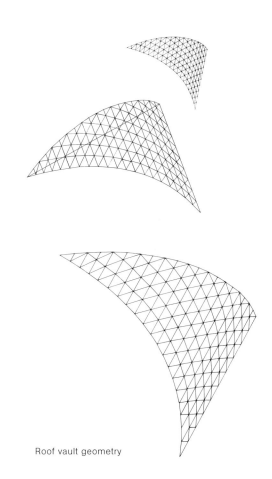

Roof vault geometry

Gallery U in Yugawara

KANAGAWA, JAPAN, 1991

The programme for this building was to create storage and exhibition rooms. This led to a simple building which is closer to a storehouse than a gallery. The materials used are very simple: exposed reinforced concrete, mortar and steel. From an early design stage the basic scheme was to anchor the storage space as a reinforced concrete box while the gallery space would be enveloped by a light vault. The original concept was of a calm empty space with softly changing colour-tones; an almost natural setting brought alive by exhibits and people, which together form small, temporary spaces. These delicately created spaces seem best surrounded and wrapped by a light, thin vaulted roof.

Usually galleries have an introverted, closed feeling, but in this particular case, considering its location and that it is a small private gallery, it is designed to have a great deal of openness.

The only space provided for display is the concrete wall of the storage box, while the other sides of the gallery space are almost non-existent, overshadowed by the vaulted roof. From the skylights and two side openings wind flows through the space and gentle natural light shifts smoothly across the gallery, forming continuity between it and the terrace. When artworks or furniture such as chairs are placed on the terrace the relationship between interior and exterior is strengthened, and the intention behind the building becomes apparent.

△ View of terrace
▷ View of roof

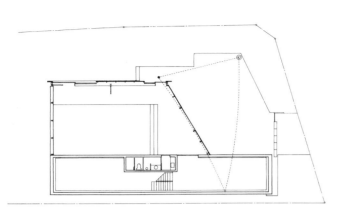

Floor plan

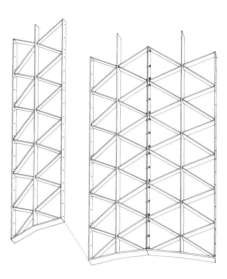

Structural detail of roof vault

△ Gallery space
← View toward outside from gallery space

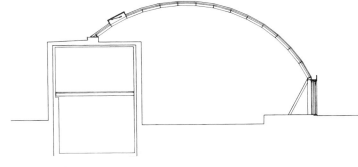

Cross section

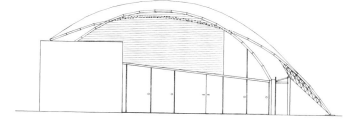

Elevation

Shimosuwa Municipal Museum

NAGANO, JAPAN 1993

◁ View of curved roof
▽ Interior view
→ Exterior at dusk

To commemorate the centennial of Shimosuwa, a city in the centre of the Nagano Prefecture, the municipal museum was reconstructed on the shores of Lake Shimosuwa. The design was selected in a competition held in June of 1990. The new museum had to accommodate two permanent collections: materials and artefacts on the history and natural environment of Lake Suwa, and a collection from the life of the famous local poet Akahiko Shimagi. The building is composed of two volumes, the permanent exhibits, which are housed on the lakeside in a linear formation, and the north storage room on the mountain side.

The walls, which follow the curve of the site, are topped with curved steel frames set every three metres, drawing the structure towards the lake. Thus a three-dimensional membrane, with arcs in plan, elevation and section, emerges to enclose the space.

The single most distinctive element is the aluminium panelling covering the front of the building, giving it the appearance of an upside-down ship floating on the Suwa Lake. This curved surface resembles the hull of the ship cutting through the water's surface. The covering is particularly welcome in the cold climate and provides a double layer of waterproofing. As with the Yatsushiro Municipal Museum and the Tower of Winds, open-jointed panels are directly attached to the steel frame as a part of the structural configuration.

Interior lighting fixtures and air-conditioning equipment are concealed in recesses in the ceilings and walls. Floor heating is provided by a supply of hot spring water, enhancing the well-controlled nature of the environment.

The scenery of the lake is projected on to a glass screen and is reflected by a thin layer of water in the courtyard, creating the rippling illusion of the exterior. The environment is therefore integrated with the building, which as a whole becomes a flowing space.

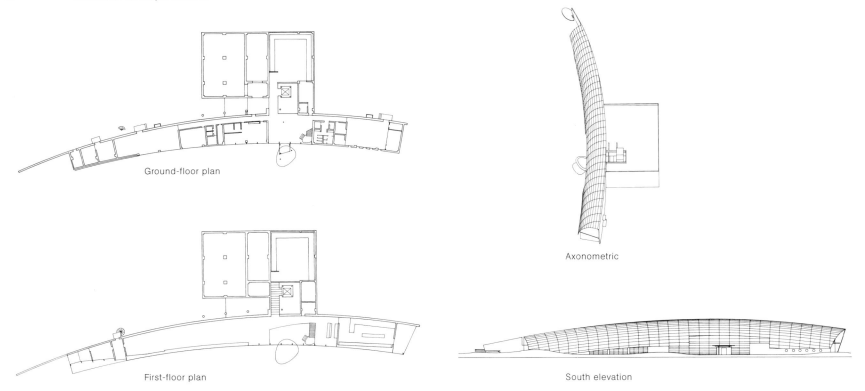

Ground-floor plan

Axonometric

First-floor plan

South elevation

△ Elevation view from Suwa Lake
← Entrance lobby

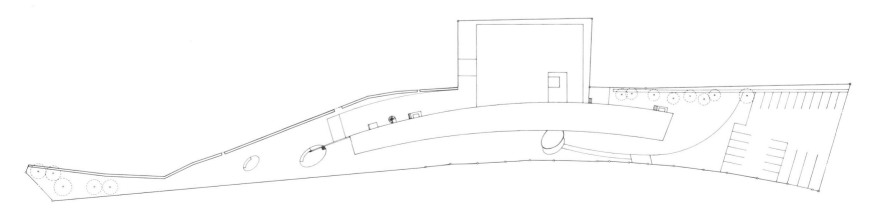

Site plan

ROOFS
WITH HOLES

Both the **Home for the Elderly in Yatsushiro** and **Yatsushiro Fire Station** were realized in the same city as the Yatsushiro Municipal Museum, through special commissions that came my way as a result of the local popularity of the museum and a commensurate increase in visitors from abroad. Drawing upon the lessons I learned from the museum, I spent much time and energy working out as completely systematized proposals as possible. The Fire Station, in a scheme reminiscent of Le Corbusier's Villa Savoye, divides functions between a tall pillared lower space for fire trucks and fire drills and the main offices above. Indeed, providing an open atrium where local citizens and especially children might watch the exciting spectacle of training and thus promote greater civic understanding of the firemen's activities was an important consideration in the spatial composition; even the upstairs offices have large semi-circular theatre-like viewing areas cut through the floor to allow observers to watch training sessions from above. In planning the Home for the Elderly, various common spaces were distributed between the rows of individual rooms in an effort to promote communication among the elderly residents. The dining hall, bathhouse, tea room, reading room, assembly rooms and studio spaces all opened in plain view on to the corridors so as to enable multiple micro-communities to thrive. Common to both these works are flat roofs dotted with skylights, creating little foci of light beneath.

The Home for the Elderly in Yatsushiro houses 50 elderly people and is located in the suburbs of Yatsushiro. The site is on reclaimed land sandwiched between the sea and an old-fashioned hot spring resort.

The two-storey building stretches 100 metres in length. Private rooms are arranged on the sides facing the streets and the common spaces such as the dining room, meeting hall and bathroom face the sea.

The building opens to both the sea and the town streets through two entrances. To ensure independence and to introduce sufficient light, common spaces with differing functions are partitioned from one another by slit-like, out-door voids that cut into the interior spaces. As the elderly residents walk along the centre corridor, they pass by and experience a sequence of different views and different aspects of their daily life. Diverse traditional floor materials such as wood, tatami and bamboo are used to evoke a feeling of nostalgia despite the modern design.

These segmented spaces are all under one large flat roof made of steel deck plates, and supported by concrete walls and slender steel pipe columns. Flat bars are inserted in between the columns at the height of the deck plate. Oval holes in the flat roof introduce the bright sunlight of Kyushu into each of the common spaces. The large common bathroom forms an independent volume enclosed by lath and polycarbonate screens.

Home for the Elderly in Yatsushiro

KUMAMOTO, JAPAN, 1994

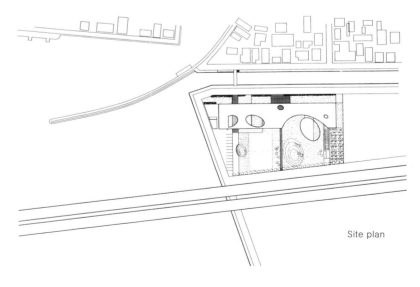

Site plan

◁ Terrace area
→ Exterior view

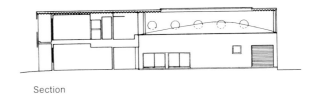

Section

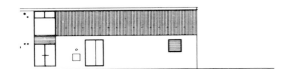

East elevation

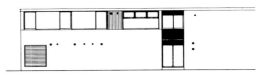

West elevation

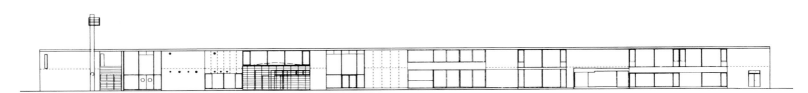

Northwest elevation

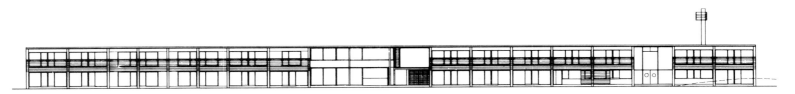

Southeast elevation

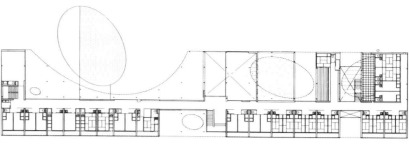

First-floor plan

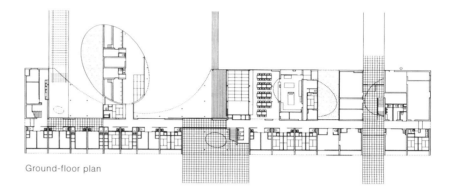

Ground-floor plan

← Assembly room and dining room
▽ Garden below large roof

Yatsushiro Fire Station

KUMAMOTO, JAPAN, 1995

This is the third public project designed by our office in Yatsushiro City, following the museum and the old people's home. The building houses the Yatsushiro Fire Station for the city and the regional headquarter offices for the branch fire stations in the district.

To preserve the spacious condition of the site, major spaces such as the offices, canteen, and sleeping quarters are arranged on the first floor, allowing most of the ground floor to be left as open space. Except for where the fire engines and ambulances are parked, the ground level is used for practice drills. Three towers and a swimming pool for rescue training and a gym for *kendo* fencing practice are laid out on the ground level. People in the community have free access to the premises to view the training sessions.

One may call the open space a park where fire extinguishing activities are staged. This is a new type of park for the public, providing the opportunity to observe the daily, though to the public unfamiliar, activities of a fire station. The use of wall structure is minimized within the design, and steel pipe columns support the structure, creating pilotis on the ground level.

The two facades facing the outer peripheral roads are linear, while the facade facing the inner park is clad in glass and curves gently. A first-floor interior corridor follows the curving profile of the facade, connecting the rooms.

The building has a very simple and clear-cut floor plan. At the same time the design carefully facilitates visual communication between the two floors.

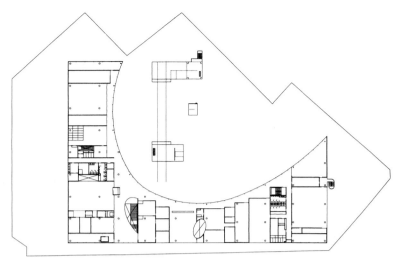

First-floor plan

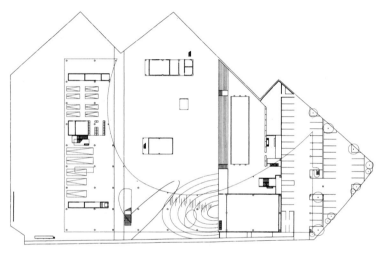

Ground-floor plan

◁ View of courtyard
→ Parking spaces on ground floor

Longitudinal section

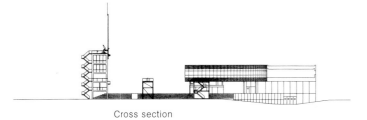

Cross section

North elevation

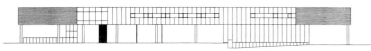

East elevation

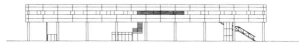

South elevation

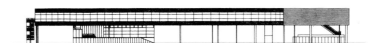

West elevation

△ Stair skylight
▷ South elevation
← Night view from courtyard

DOME

Odate is a small city of 60,000 people in the far north of Honshu, where heavy snow makes it impossible to enjoy outdoor sports for half the year. The plan was to construct a dome to allow local citizens to play baseball and football during the long winter months. From the very outset of the competition, our team proposed a structural system made of locally grown Japanese cedar laminate timbers. To withstand the severe weather conditions and weight of 1.5 metre deep snow drifts, we engineered giant 180 metre span, curved wood trusses and thus realized the largest wooden dome of its kind in the world. The **Odate Jukai Dome** is distinguished not only by its wood construction, but also its shape: the ovoid form was a concession to the winds that blow from the same direction all year round. Cool breezes blow in over a rainwater pond in the summer, while the curvature of the dome is designed to prevent whirlwinds during winter snowstorms. The wooden truss assembly fits on to a supporting concrete tension ring and is covered with a double-layered translucent teflon film that lets in natural light during the day and glows from within after sunset like a gigantic lamp in the snow. The whole structure, moreover, is raised on concrete columns to bring a continuous view of the environment inside. Our greatest design concern, however, was to ensure that this new man-made scenic wonder responded in a most natural way to the beautiful Snow Country landscape. The Dome changes in appearance hour by hour throughout the day and when viewed from different directions it is a surprisingly harmonious complement to the surrounding hills.

Odate Jukai Dome

AKITA, JAPAN, 1997

Odate City, together with the mountainous regions of northern Akita Prefecture and the cities of Noshiro and Takasu along the Yoneshiro River, has a booming business in lumber and composite materials processing. For some time proposals have been afloat to find a way to improve the local economy by developing new ways to exploit the local cedar forests. The far side of the site opens up to a view of the mountains stretching off into the distance and a beautiful natural environment including a forest of deciduous trees. Unfortunately, however, Odate is also a place of long, snow-bound winters. Our goal then in continuing the planning process was to propose a structure that would take this natural environment seriously.

The dome shape was adopted as the result of a combination of factors, including the southwesterly winds that blow all year round from the Yoneshiro River, aerodynamic considerations with regard to the snow, the arch of the baseball in flight and the circulation of air inside the structure. For the structure of the dome, we employed a two-directional arch truss made of composite materials from local cedar; a product of nature both in terms of form and material.

The dome is unified with nature, lightly covering the surface of the earth and creating an environment that gives a sense of great openness and connection with the pond, field, green hills, and deciduous forest.

In order to create a natural interior environment even in the harsh winter climate, a teflon membrane was employed to introduce natural light. At night the dome glows softly like the moon from the light within, creating an entirely new vista.

△ View of playing field and
roof structure
← View across Yoneshiro river

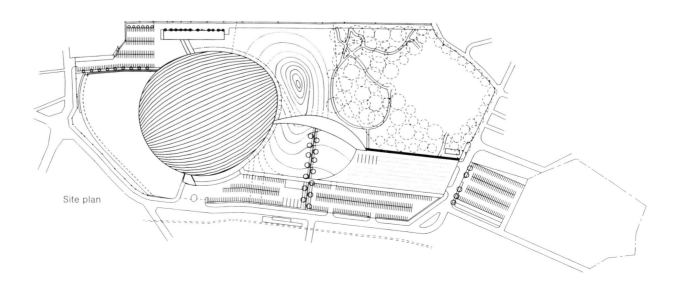

Site plan

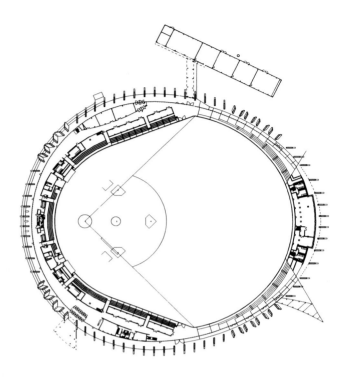

Ground-floor plan

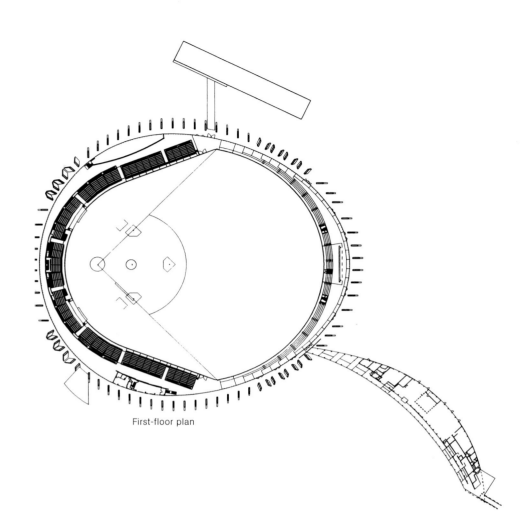

First-floor plan

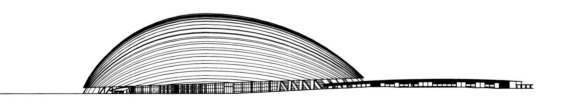

Southeast elevation

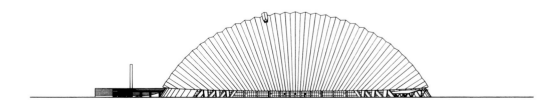

Southwest elevation

△ Night view
→ Following pages: View of roof structure

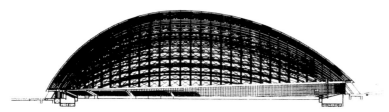

Northwest section

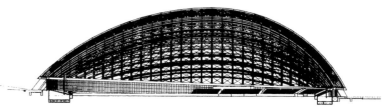

Southeast section

THEATRES

In addition to the three theatre and concert hall projects presented here, we are working on a theatre complex in the Koenji district of Tokyo and an opera theatre complex in Taipei. Theatre is one of the most common experiences we share within public buildings, yet paradoxically the more we know, the more difficult it becomes to plan performance halls in an original way. In the 1990s, we tried to de-programme public buildings or even inject wholly new programmatic conditions in order to break out of the status quo planning mould, but performing arts venues are not so easy to rethink; theatres and concert halls all have such clear precedents—shoebox hall, proscenium stage—corresponding to established modes of presentation, while the specific requirements for acoustics and visibility largely dictate audience seating configurations. The **Nagaoka Lyric Hall** was our first venture into performance-hall design, so we were especially mindful of standard theatre formats, although one unique feature we adopted was a foyer space that acts as a fluid intermediating zone between the various halls. The **T Hall in Shimane** comprises a library and two halls. While the halls themselves are conventional in design, we strove to accommodate a wide range of use situations by incorporating a stepped foyer alongside the large hall, and an outdoor terrace. The **Matsumoto Performing Arts Centre** pairs a large U-shaped hall of sufficient scale for opera together with a more flexible small hall that can adapt to more free-form performances. Both halls are fairly straightforward in plan, yet by adding a broad foyer space, rehearsal rooms and an adjoining roof-top garden we have greatly increased the possibilities for hosting more diverse expressions.

This complex includes a 700-seat concert hall, a 450-seat theatre and 10 studios of various sizes. The site is located in the cultural and educational zone of Nagaoka City, in an immensely vast and flat landscape that in turn emphasizes the infinite expanse of the sky. Since Nagaoka City already has a multipurpose hall seating 1,500 people, the two halls in this complex are intended exclusively for musical and theatrical performances. With well-equipped studios open to the public, the complex serves as a base for cultural and artistic activities where people can actively participate instead of being a mere audience.

Since there was sufficient space on the site, the buildings have a low (two-storey) profile. The two volumes with oval and rectangle forms in plan are, respectively, the concert hall and the theatre. Other sections of the complex are covered with a gently undulating vaulted roof. The gentle slope of the grass-covered mound leads to the foyer on the south side of the complex.

The corrugated glass wall enveloping the concert hall protects the inside from the noise of the bypass road to the north of the site. At twilight, the glass wall glows with light from the interior, turning the hall into a landmark. The expansive roof seems to assimilate with the surrounding mountains, and the grass-covered mound stretches in clear contrast to the two projecting volumes behind, creating a man-made naturalistic landscape in the otherwise non-descript site. The vast roof that covers the foyer, studios and information lounge has a reinforced concrete non-beam plate structure. Rays of light shower the complex between pillars in random arrangements, from the courtyard and through holes piercing the roof, creating the atmosphere of a forest. The concert hall is designed as a single box with an oval plan. The shape of the hall and the two rows of balcony seats on both sides of the stage emphasize a feeling of unity between the audience and the performers. The rectangular-shaped second hall is a theatre with a proscenium stage and the simplest spatial planning possible in order not to impair the directional freedom of the stage. The theatre features advanced technical facilities comparable to the finest theatres in the metropolitan area.

The complex plays a significant role in the community as a place for a variety of cultural activities open to the public.

Nagaoka Lyric Hall

NIIGATA, JAPAN, 1996

△ West passage to concert hall
▷ Exterior at dusk
← Courtyard view

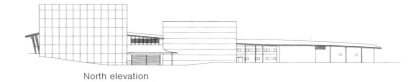

North elevation

East elevation

West elevation

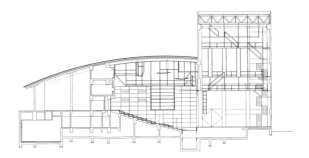

Section through theatre

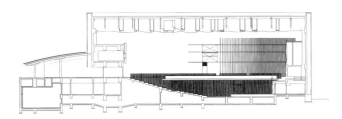

Section through hall

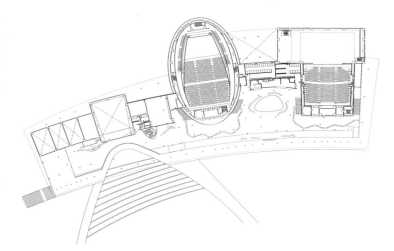

First-floor plan

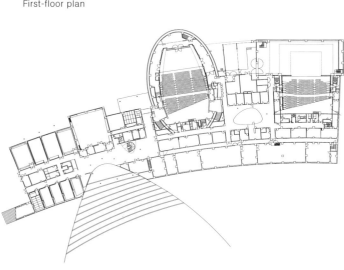

Ground-floor plan

△ Night view
▷ Communal space and
  entrance to concert hall
← Concert hall

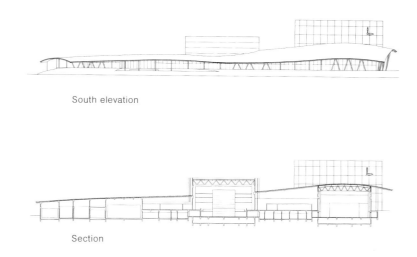

South elevation

Section

T Hall in Shimane

SHIMANE, JAPAN, 1999

This project is a complex including a main hall (600 fixed seats), multipurpose hall (200 movable seats), library, conference room and study room. It was originally designed for Kabuki plays, however, in accordance with the city administration's wishes, the programme of the facility switched to become mainly a multipurpose hall complex with a library. The main objective of the project was to re-establish the area of the site as an important cultural zone in the city. The site was also designed to be pedestrian friendly with walkways built to link back to the city hall and other municipal buildings.

One of the most frequent topics of discussion during the design process was the definition of the halls and the characteristics of their spatial envelope. In order to moderate the solid feeling typical of the conventional hall, prefabricated panels of reinforced concrete were used in place of thick cast concrete walls. In the main hall, double-layered vertical glass openings were left between the panels, allowing natural light to filter into the space. The round plan of the smaller hall facilitates flexible rearrangements in layout, accommodating a variety of functions. Similar strategies to blur spatial and functional boundaries were also employed at the entrance to the lobby of the halls and with the library.

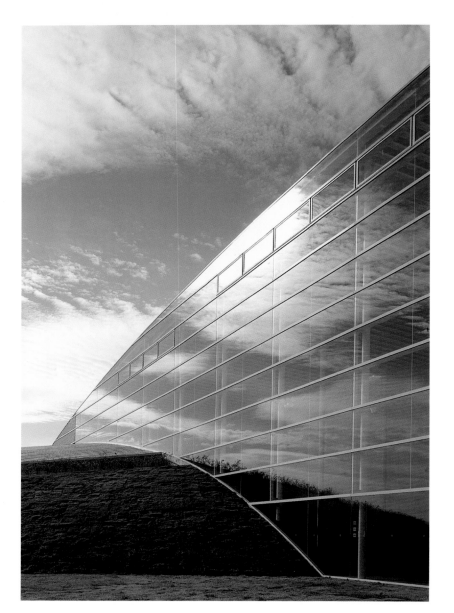

△ Night view of eastern glass facade
← View of roof from south
← Eastern glass facade

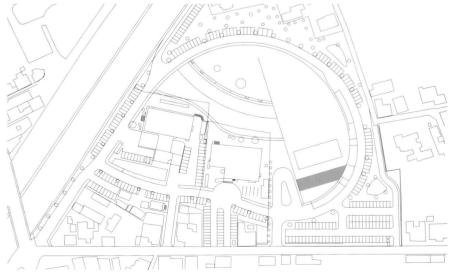

Site plan

→ Open stack library
→ Multipurpose hall
▽ Hall terrace

Section

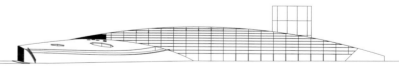

East elevation

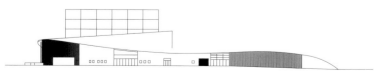

South elevation

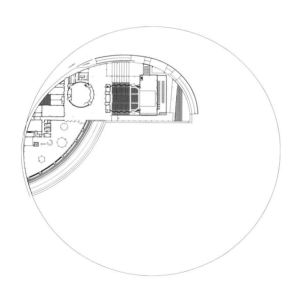

Ground-floor plan

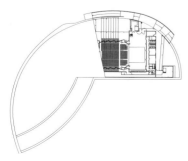

Basement plan

The Matsumoto Performing Arts Centre is comprised of one small and one large performance hall and is located in Matsumoto City, Nagano Prefecture, on the site of the former theatre in the city centre. The plan was drawn up for a competition among ten design teams. The larger hall, which seats 1,800, was required to accommodate opera performances for the annual summer Saito Kinen Festival, as well as a variety of theatrical performances and other events. Smaller local events and citizens' meetings are housed in the more intimate space of the 240-seat hall. In addition, the facility includes rehearsal rooms and studios that serve as venues for a wide variety of activities.

The biggest challenge was in finding a way to fit the programme into an unusually shaped site that stretches from north to south like a wine bottle. The site width and other conditions, including the diagonal placement of the road, necessitated that the larger hall run along the southern side of the site. Although intuitively this would have placed the stage at the back edge of the site, such a configuration would turn the back of the building toward the residential area to the south. After studying a variety of patterns, we came up with the idea of turning the hall around and placing the stage in the centre. This configuration places the seating area and surrounding foyer on the south side of the site,

alleviating the problem of front and back with respect to the neighbouring residential area. An entrance with a gentle sloping staircase into the foyer and the smaller hall were then placed along the site's northern edge and a lobby space for relaxing was inserted between the large and small halls. By reversing the direction of the large hall we were able to create a fluid design without a front or a back, transforming the architecture into a park-like space.

Initially, for the competition, we proposed a milky-white double-glass glazing for the building. After beginning the actual design process, however, we realized that the surroundings were not uniformly attractive and that the interior spatial sequence leading up to the theatre deserved a more remarkable and inspiring facade. We wanted something that used the same system and materials to create lighting responsive to a variety of situations, and which would give not a geometric impression, but a random and natural one. The fibreglass reinforced concrete panels that we finally chose introduce soft light into the interior through randomly inlaid glass. The lighting shifts according to the amount of glass and the orientation of the outer walls to create a variety of places within a fluid and continuous space, beckoning visitors on towards the theatre.

Matsumoto Performing Arts Centre

NAGANO, JAPAN, 2004

◁ Close-up of inlaid glass
→ Exterior view of glass-inlaid panels

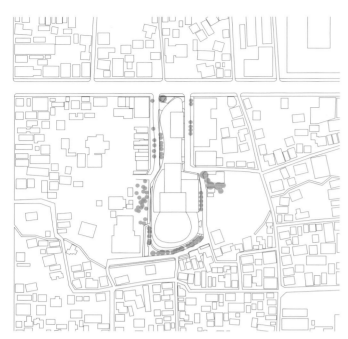

Site plan

125

⌂ Roof-top garden
← View from south

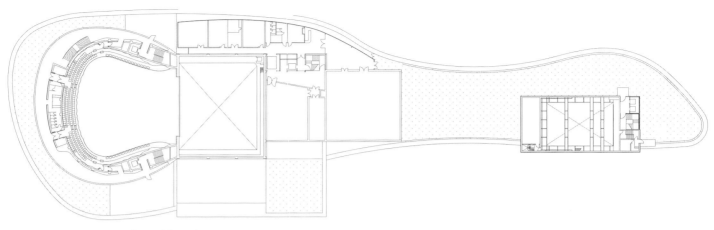

Second-floor plan

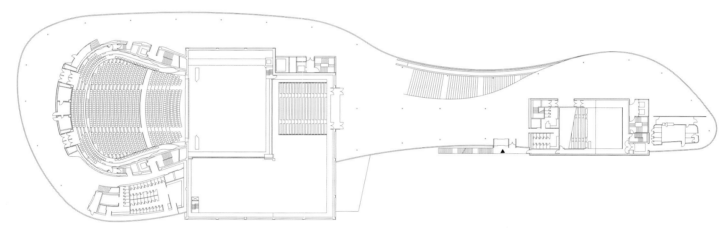

First-floor plan

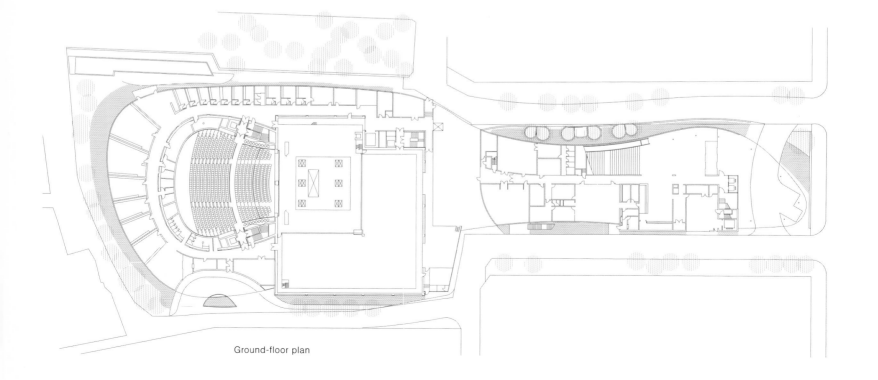

Ground-floor plan

△ Main stair from entrance
→ Following pages: View down main stair

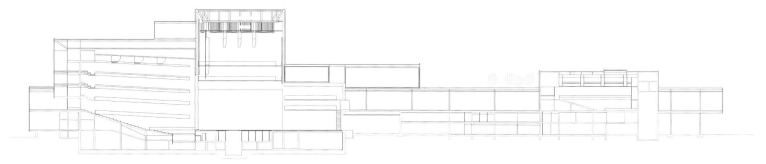

Longitudinal section

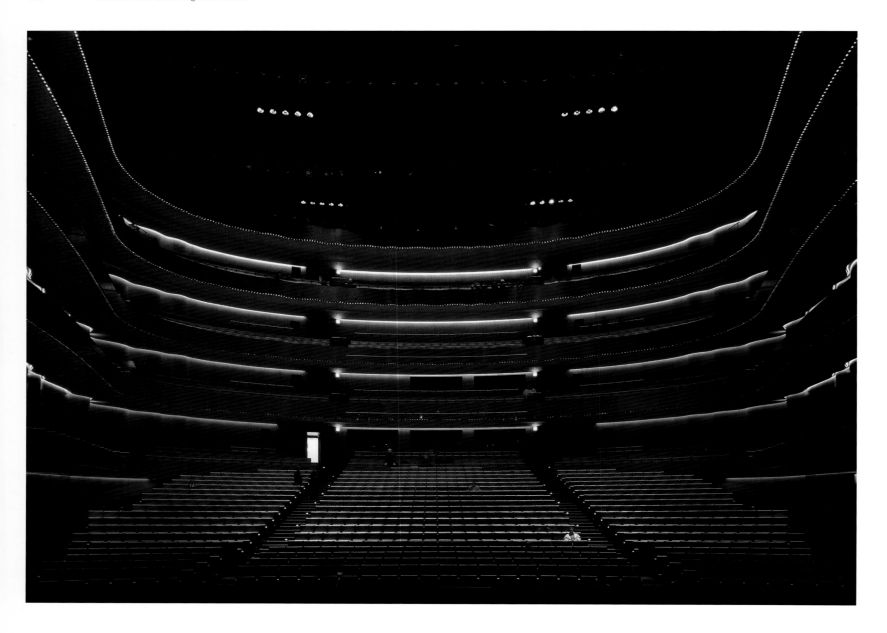

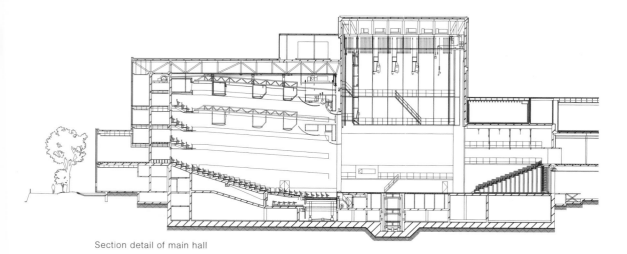

Section detail of main hall

▷ Tiered hall seating
▽ Stage view from roll-back seating
← Interior view of large hall

MEDIATHEQUE/
LIBRARY

The **Sendai Mediatheque** was surely one of the high points of my career as an architect. It gave me a great sense of fulfilment to finally be able to realize my architectural ideas of many years, and helped to take those ideas to the next level. The building greeted the dawn of the new millennium with a countdown to zero hour on 1 January 2000, when the big glass doors in front opened and in rushed throngs of cheering people, since when about a million people annually have been using the facility. The Mediatheque differs from conventional public buildings in many ways. While the building principally functions as a library and art gallery, the administration has actively worked to relax divisions between diverse programmes, removing fixed barriers between various media to progressively evoke an image of how cultural facilities should be from now on. This openness is the direct result of its simple structure, consisting of flat concrete slabs penetrated by 13 tubes. Walls on each floor are kept to an absolute minimum, allowing the various functions to be freely distributed throughout the open areas between the tubes. Moreover, each floor differs in ceiling height to further diversify the spaces, while the slanting tubes break up the interiors in different ways, adding visual interest, as well as making the public and staff alike feel simultaneously uninhibited yet united. The spatial strength delivered by the welded steel-plate, honeycomb slab structural system also proved a major influence on my architectural planning thereafter. More specifically a library than Sendai, the **Tama Art University Library (Hachioji Campus)** employs a different structural system, although not without certain similarities. Half the space of the ground floor is given over to a foyer-like open passageway whose concrete floor conforms to the 1:20 incline of the site, a multipurpose 'salon' where students and faculty can mount exhibitions or hold lectures. Even within the library, the relaxed ground-floor spaces for watching DVDs or browsing magazines are comparable to the first two floors of Sendai. Tama is quite unlike Sendai, however, in that its alternating concrete arches describe a rhythmic continuity while articulating the upper-floor reading room, although the possibility of reading anywhere follows up on concepts from Sendai. Steel-plate cores give these arches their lightness and delicacy. Here, then, is a compendium of the many new construction and structural techniques we introduced from Sendai onwards.

The Sendai Mediatheque stands along Jozenji street, a main avenue in Sendai famous for its stately rows of zelkova trees. Completed in August 2000, five and a half years after the open competition held by Sendai City, this project rises 8 storeys from ground level with 21,600 square metres in total floor space.

In the early stages of planning, four different functions were proposed for the facility: an art gallery, a library, a visual image media centre and a service centre for people with visual or hearing disabilities. During the competition, however, we were asked to combine these programmes together and show a revolutionary form of architecture. From the competition through the basic design process, our main objective was to break free from conventional art museum or library archetypes; we carefully analysed each programme, eventually re-composing them to create a 'Mediatheque'. The basic design was developed through consultation with specialists from various fields and through numerous hearings for the exchange of opinions with Sendai's citizens.

Since such discussions are endless, flexibility is required in the architectural 'hardware' that can respond to any development or can accommodate any programme in the future. We did not change our idea after the competition; rather than a formalist architecture, ours is a simple yet conceptual proposal consisting of three plain elements: 'plate', 'tube' and 'skin'.

The 'plate' element is a place to enhance the different forms of communication between people or between people and things. The ground floor opens to the outside with a café, shops and square. On the first floor, plentiful newspapers, magazines and computers allow people to browse and get information. The library is on the second and third floors, where patrons can browse and borrow books from the open stacks. The fourth and fifth floors are both gallery spaces of differing ceiling height and spatial characters; the fourth floor is divided into small spaces, while the fifth is separated by movable partitions. The sixth floor is a space for visual media and creation, where film viewing and workshops take place.

Thirteen tree-like 'tube' elements penetrate vertically through the plates. Built from lattices of steel pipes and ranging from 2 to 9 metres in diameter, the tubes are not only flexible as structural elements, but also spaces where information and different types of energy (light, air, water, sound, etc.) flow while facilitating vertical circulation. Through the action of these tubes, fields are generated by the natural and electronic flows within the uniform space of the 'plates'.

The 'skin' refers to the envelope that separates the interior of the architecture from the exterior. The concept for the double-skin facade facing the main street is particularly important.

The Mediatheque is composed of these three elements and few fixed walls, allowing each floor to be expressed as one large 50 square metre room. The rooms are divided into many undetermined spaces by the tubes, and visitors may freely pass time in anyway and anywhere they like.

Since opening in January 2001, the Mediatheque has attracted up to 2,000 people daily with its lively urban plaza-like atmosphere, and serves as a symbol of public space for the citizens of Sendai.

Sendai Mediatheque

MIYAGI, JAPAN, 2000

▷ View upward inside a tube
→ Night view

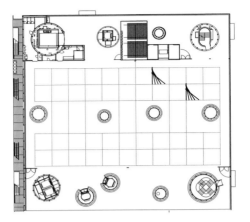

Fifth-floor plan

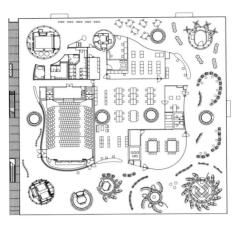

Sixth-floor plan

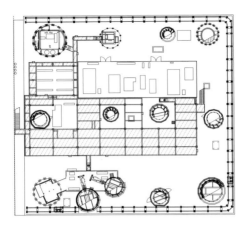

Roof plan

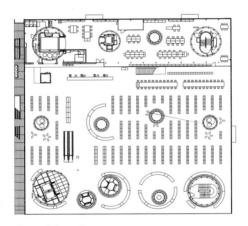

Second-floor plan

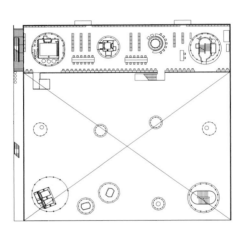

Third-floor plan

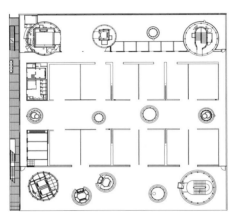

Fourth-floor plan

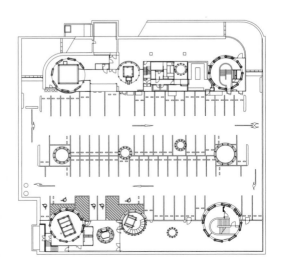

Basement plan

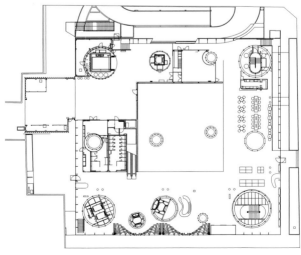

Ground-floor plan

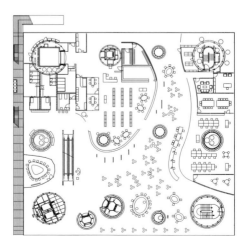

First-floor plan

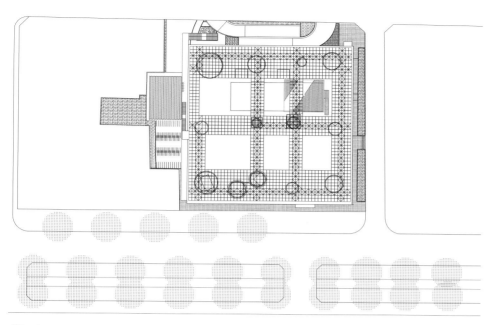

Site plan

▽ Street view from southwest

▵ Exterior night view
▷ Reading desks around a tube in library
← Ground-floor café
← First-floor newspaper and magazine browsing area

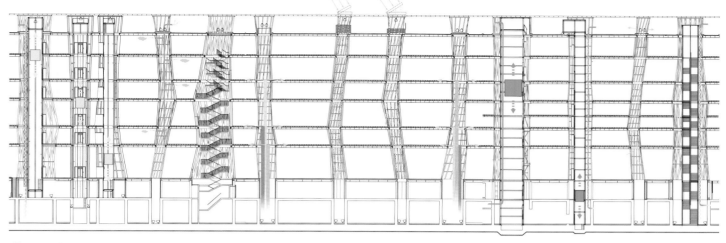

The tubes function variously as housing for stairs
and lifts, air conditioning and light wells

← View downward through a tube
▽ Second-floor window benches in library

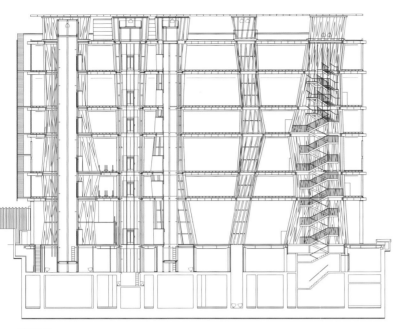

Section

→ View through a tube
▽ Street view from southeast at night

This is a library for an art university located in the suburbs of Tokyo. Facing the main entrance gate, the site lies behind a front garden with trees and stretches up a gentle slope.

In addition to enriching the library space for the entire campus, from the early stages of planning it was strongly requested that we create a space capable of enhancing communication between students and professors.

Our first idea was to create a wide-open gallery space on the ground level separate from the library that would serve as an active thoroughfare for people crossing the campus on the way to other buildings. This gallery has the same grade as the site and creates the sensation that the sloping terrain and the front garden's scenery continue within the building. The space can be used for lectures and performances, and as a café where students can get together and relax.

Series of continuous but asymmetrical concrete arches shroud both floors, crisscrossing each other as they trace curved lines. To minimize the thickness of these arches we adopted a special structural system in which central steel plates are sandwiched on both sides by a layer of concrete. This construction system allowed the cross-joint columns to connect to the ground in an extremely slim shape; the spans of the arches vary from 1.8 to 16 metres, but the thickness is kept to a uniform 200 mm. The space is gently divided by the crossing of the arches, yet remains continuous. Bookshelves and reading tables with undulating forms stretch through the space.

Tama Art University Library (Hachioji Campus)

TOKYO, JAPAN, 2007

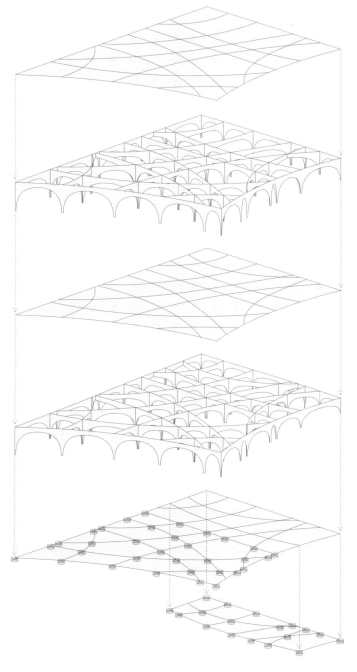

→ Open stacks and reading area
→ Following pages: First-floor reading area

Diagram of column and arch structure

△ Multimedia browsing area
▷ Café
◄ Main entrance lobby
◄ Open stack and reading area with low bookshelves

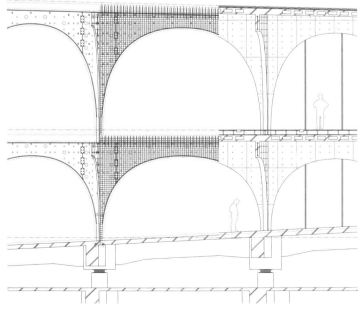

△ Night view of ground-floor public areas from exterior

← Night view of south facade

Construction allowing for seismic activity

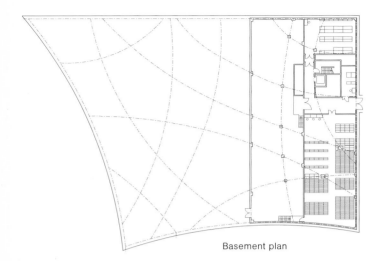

Basement plan

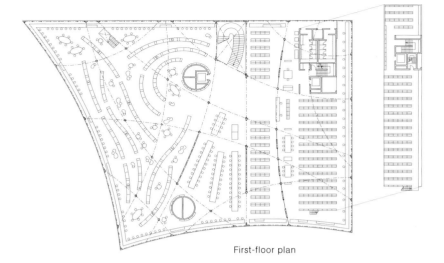

First-floor plan

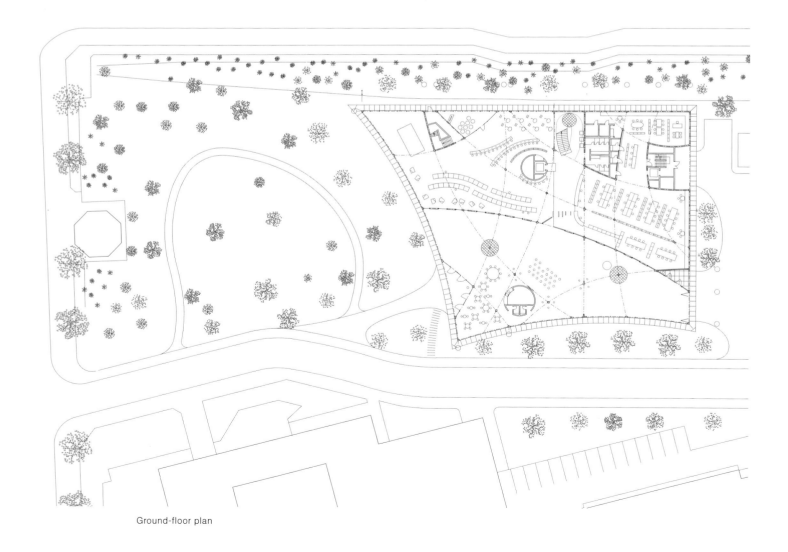

Ground-floor plan

△ View of facade from southwest corner

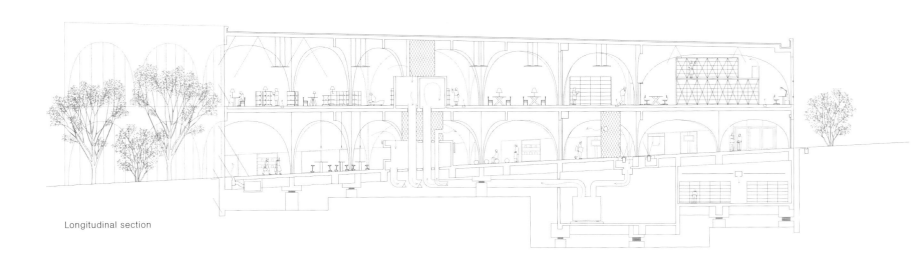

Longitudinal section

◁ East facade at night
▽ West facade
→ View of entrance

PAVILIONS

In 2002, we made temporary pavilions in two European cities: a **Bruges Pavilion** in Belgium aided by Masato Araya and a **Serpentine Gallery Pavilion 2002** in London realized in collaboration with Cecil Balmond. Their genius at structural engineering allowed us to create structural systems that would themselves function as surface designs, a scheme that helped to inspire such later large-scale works as TOD'S Omotesando and MIKIMOTO Ginza 2. While both Pavilions basically explore the same direction, they differ markedly in character. In Bruges, we utilized an aluminium structure to a light and ephemeral effect. Whatever we built was not to disturb the historic foundations of the original cathedral, an important civic symbol, underlying the town square, so the pavilion needed to be physically lightweight. We made a gate-shaped structure entirely out of aluminium honeycomb core material and affixed elliptical aluminium panels inside and out for reinforcement. Then we shaved away both sides of those areas on the honeycomb blocks with no ellipses to render the mass virtually transparent, although arguably it also weakened the structure. This intentional weakening helped to heighten the ephemeral appearance. The Serpentine, on the other hand, was articulated out of linear elements to form a cube structure of surfaces only. Taking what ordinarily would have been a grid-form horizontal plane and algorithmically rotating concentric squares within it, then extending those lines down the vertical faces, we generated a rotational form enlivened by spatial rhythms that avoided typical Euclidian geometries and so created a curiously dynamic 'impossible object'. This dynamism was its fascination.

Bruges is a beautiful city in Belgium surrounded by water and famous for its well-preserved streets from medieval times. The city was designated a 'cultural capital' of the European Union in 2002. In the same year, this pavilion was built in the central square to serve as a symbol of the city.

When this project began, like many other ancient cities in Europe, Bruges was striving to solve the contradictory demands of the city: preserving the historical urban landscape while enhancing its potential as a modern city. For this project, we were asked to show the potential of new architecture in this historical urban context. Specific functions were not required for the building and it was only requested that the building become a symbol appropriate for a cultural capital.

We proposed building an aluminium pavilion that contrasts with the masonry buildings of the medieval city. We designed a gate-shaped tunnel with a honeycomb structure. Since this structure was too weak to support itself, we added a minimal number of aluminium panels on both the inside and outside in order to reinforce the structure. The panels were arranged like floating islands and the loads between the panels were distributed to the honey-comb structure between the panels. In contrast to the seriousness of the structural analysis performed, the pattern of floating islands looks rather playful, like paper cutouts.

Keeping in mind that the historic ruins of a medieval church are buried just below this site, we designed a shallow circular pond that reflects the shape of its foundation. We then put a floating bridge made of resin across the pond and gently installed the semi-transparent aluminium frames on top of it, lending the structure the effect of floating on water.

Surrounded by water, and sitting in the centre of this historical city, this half transparent aluminium pavilion was brought in somewhat unexpectedly and changed the mood of the square dramatically. At the same time, however, the surface of the pavilion resembles the traditional lace-work craft of this town, forming a unique harmony with the historical urban landscape.

Traditional Belgian lace

Bruges Pavilion

BRUGES, BELGIUM, 2002

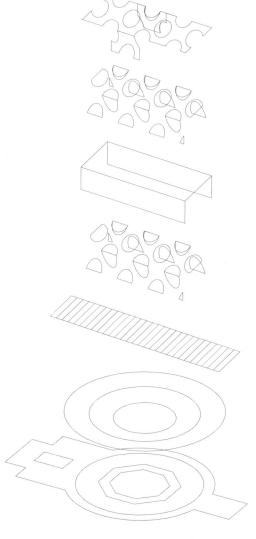

Composition diagram

→ Interior view

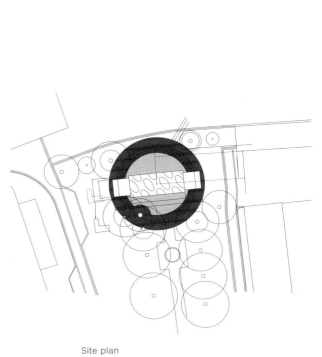

Site plan

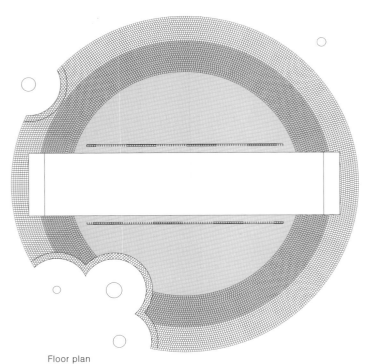

Floor plan

△ South elevation
◄ View toward plaza
  from pavilion

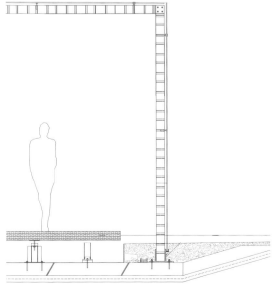

Sectional detail

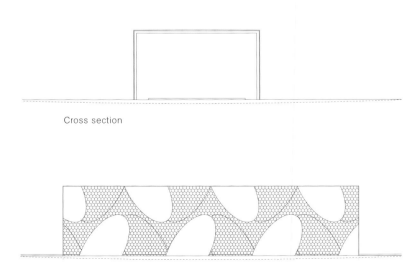

Cross section

Elevation

Serpentine Gallery Pavilion 2002

LONDON, GREAT BRITAIN, 2002

This temporary pavilion stood in front of the Serpentine Gallery in Kensington Gardens, London, for three months during the summer of 2002. Every day many visitors filled the pavilion, relaxing at the café during the day, and using the space for parties, debates and lectures after sunset. It had a box-like shape, 18 by 18 metres in plan and 4.5 metres in height, and no internal columns.

In collaboration with the structural engineer Cecil Balmond of Arup, we developed a structural lattice system of steel flat bars for the project. Although the structure may appear random at first glance, it is actually a spiral pattern, which is based upon an algorithm for an expanding and rotating square. Since the elements in the system share a complex interdependence with each other, overall structural equilibrium is maintained. The structure is continuous from wall to roof and the 550 mm wide steel plates are adjusted in thickness from 12 to 50 mm according to the local structural stress.

The surface is tiled in a chequered pattern of aluminium panels and glass. This abstract polygonal pattern, derived by cutting the surface along the lines of the structure, lent an upbeat and lively mood to the gallery lawn. Although the pavilion was disassembled after three months, it has since been sold and rebuilt at Battersea Power Station, on the bank of the Thames in south-west London.

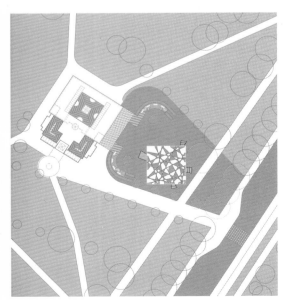

Site plan

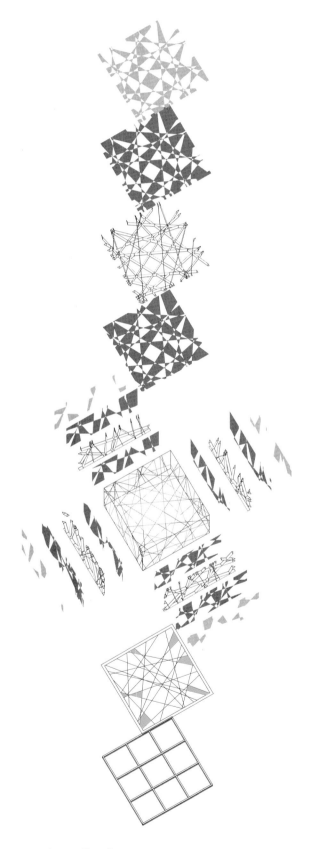

Composition diagram

△ Exterior view

Unfolded elevation

△ View of southeast corner
← Pavilion in use
← Interior view

Floor plan

ALUMINIUM
STRUCTURES

While not as strong as steel and ill-suited for large-scale structures, aluminium offers unique possibilities as a structural material for smaller residential-scale projects. First of all, aluminium is light: at only a third the specific gravity of steel, two people can generally carry any framing element, hence it can facilitate construction on sites inaccessible to cranes. Next, aluminium bars (posts, beams) can be readily extruded with the utmost precision to create complicated cross-sectional shapes similar to those of window sashes. It is even possible to make posts that also serve as sash uprights and combination beam/sash crossbars, thereby eliminating the distinction between structural members and finishing elements. Thus, extruded aluminium framing reverses Modernist architecture's industrialized division of structure from cosmetic finish. If anything, this probably runs closer to automotive thinking or moulded product manufacturing. One seemingly 'retro' approach we call the 'aluminium brick method', which we used to design the **Aluminium Brick Housing in Groningen,** takes hollow, brick-sized cross-sections of extruded rectangular bars and stacks them like masonry, essentially recreating pre-modern construction in aluminium. Or again, we've already done two projects – **Aluminium Cottage** and the **Dormitory for SUS Company Fukushima Branch** – using high-precision extrusion techniques to create honeycombed or ribbed panels (walls, roofing) with innovative joint detailing that snaps together to form continuous surfaces without additional adhesives or sealants. We are presently conducting in-house experiments using these quick-sealing elements toward such applications as 'remedy housing' in response to 'sick house syndrome'.

This is a development project for an aluminium cottage. Given the premise to develop general housing using aluminium, our main strategy was to create a prototype of a small cottage with a relatively simple plan.

The humid climate of the site presented the problem of possible corrosion to the exterior surfaces and the internal structure of the building if maintenance is not periodically carried out.

Thus, we sought to develop a maintenance-free cottage that acts as a shelter when its shutters are closed, and makes the most effective use of aluminium's high corrosion resistance.

This project has a total floor area of 74.4 square metres. The partly two-storey volume has a shed roof and a fan-shape in plan. The unique shape, like a 'tetrapak' with trimmed edges, is created with the plan and elevation arranged as inverses to each other. This allows the whole building to be composed using a single extrusion moulding aluminium panel module with the same cross-section. To trim the panels of the roof, walls and floor, only one cutting angle is necessary, significantly simplifying the manufacturing process.

Only five extrusion mouldings were used. The total material weight of aluminium, including floors and plinths, was 4.9 tons; a remarkably lightweight building. All of the components are light enough to be carried by two workers, thereby making it possible to construct it without any machinery, much like a log house in a mountainous region. Moreover, the construction period was shortened dramatically thanks to its lightness. The construction was completed in about 55 days.

The aluminium panels are conceived of not only as structural members but also as the exterior material. In the simple joint connections between panels, water resistance is ensured by the high precision of the extrusions. Panels join together perfectly like a intricate mosaic to make a perfectly flat surface. This simple connection method makes the work on-site much easier and facilitates any future dismantling and reconstruction work.

In this experimental project, 32 U-shaped panels were arranged along the longitudinal direction to build the cottage. However, the outer dimensions can be altered flexibly by adding or subtracting panels of 300 mm width. Furthermore, depending on the required spatial volume and budget considerations, the form of the building can vary by changing the cross-section of aluminium elements.

Aluminium architecture has multifaceted potential and we have been exploring new possibilities. As a touchstone, the aluminium cottage project still stands in the green mountains.

Aluminium Cottage

YAMANASHI, JAPAN, 2004

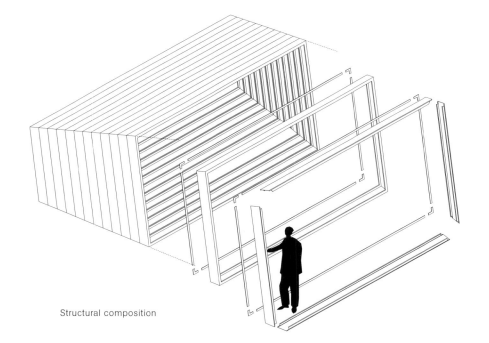

Structural composition

→ View from west

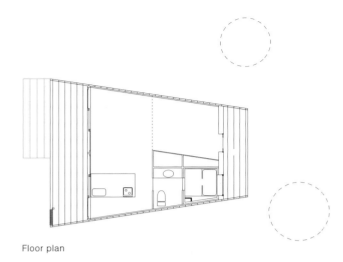

Floor plan

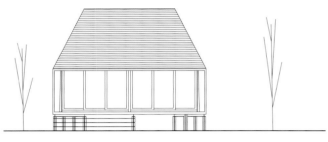

West elevation

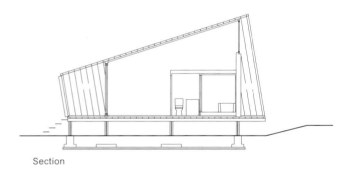

Section

East elevation

◁ View toward entrance
→ Interior view
→ View from garden

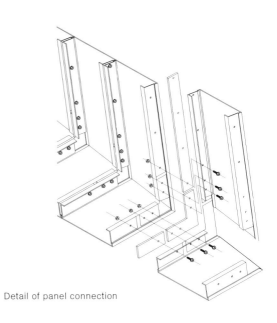

Detail of panel connection

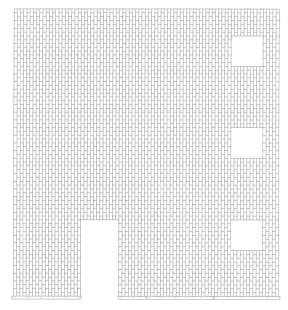

Elevation

Aluminium Brick Housing in Groningen

GRONINGEN, NETHERLANDS, 2005

As a part of the event 'Blue-Moon project', held in the Dutch city of Groningen, five architects were asked to design a house among the traditional architecture of the beautifully preserved old centre of the city. In consideration for the short period of time for construction and the importance of symbolizing the character of the event, we proposed student housing with an extruded aluminium rigid-frame structure.

However, during the detailed design phase of the project, the site and programme had to be modified significantly for a variety of reasons.

The new site was located adjacent to a historic library, which was made of bricks, and we were requested to connect our design with this old building. We decided to use reinforced-concrete slabs and columns for the main structure, and an aluminium framework in a brick-pattern was developed to form a sash system that supports the glass facade. The brick-shaped extruded aluminium units were assembled together and incorporated into the three-story facade, supporting the exterior glass, while resisting the wind load. The light and transparent aluminium brick facade is connected to the brick masonry of the adjoining dignified building, therefore both unifying and contrasting the buildings, and creating a unique expression in the cityscape.

△ Aluminium brick-pattern facade from exterior
▷ Interior view
◀ View along street

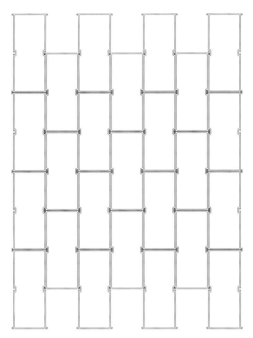

Detail of aluminum brick-pattern panel

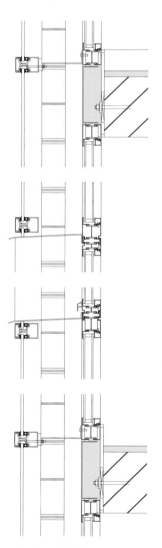

Sectional detail

175

△ Facade from interior
← Detail of facade
← View along street from entrance

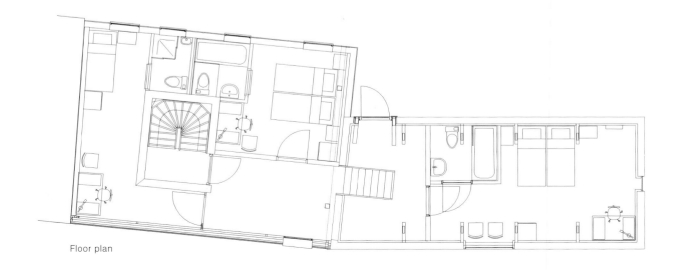

Floor plan

Site plan

This building is a company dormitory for 'business bachelors' who work at the SUS factory in the Prefecture of Fukushima, Japan. The SUS Corporation manufactures automation devices for factories, and recently has actively expanded its business into the field of aluminium building materials. Since this dormitory also serves as a guesthouse for clients and visitors, the most important theme for us was to demonstrate that an aluminium structure could be highly suitable for living in.

In contrast to the image of aluminium being hard and flat, we wanted to create an expression of softness and curviness. Fifteen rows of gently curved walls were built using R-shaped extruded aluminium components. And on top of the walls, we installed these same aluminium components to form the roof structure.

These curved aluminium walls gently divide the space, defining the bedrooms and common spaces within the units. Aside from the aluminium walls and the roof of the main structure, we used wooden materials for many parts of the building, including the fixtures. By juxtaposing aluminium and wood, we sought to create a rich and unique spatial experience.

There are nine bedrooms, and the common spaces between these rooms are used in a variety of ways, such as places for talking, reading over tea, areas for strolling around, or even as a gallery for displaying company products. In good weather, these spaces can be opened up to the exterior. To heat the aluminium walls, we adopted an active radiant heating system.

This aluminium housing which has a warm and soft atmosphere might suggest a new form of living space. Residents continue to live comfortably in this housing.

Dormitory for SUS Company Fukushima Branch

FUKUSHIMA, JAPAN, 2005

Floor plan

→ View between curved walls

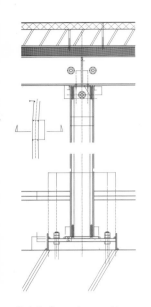
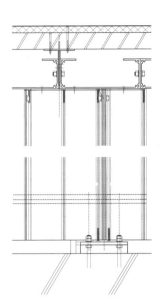
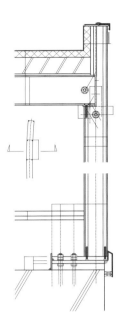

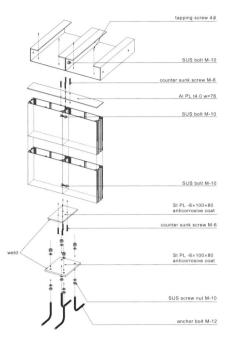

tapping screw 4φ

SUS bolt M-10

counter sunk screw M-6

Al PL t4.0 w=76

SUS bolt M-10

SUS bolt M-10

St PL -6×100×80
anticorrosive coat

counter sunk screw M-6

weld

St PL -6×100×80
anticorrosive coat

SUS screw nut M-10

anchor bolt M-12

Detail of panel assembly

Structural parts composition diagram

△ View from road
▷ Interior view of a room
← View of entrance
→ Following pages: View from garden

△ Night view from exterior
▷ Night view of dining space from exterior
← View along corridor
← View of dining space

URBAN
NURTURE

The project for a terminal care hospice in Paris, **Hospital Cognacq-Jay in Paris,** intended to offer a restful environment for patients to live out their last days, comprises mostly minimal size bedrooms to provide basic functions with little in the way of furnishings or interior design. Within such stringent conditions, the most crucial question was how to create an architecture of peace and quiet in relation to, yet independent from, the urban environment. The 15th Arrondissement site occupies a block immediately adjacent to housing and a hospital. The existing century-old structures on the grounds were laden with history but chaotic, so we wanted to reinstate something of the *quartier* as it originally was in the form of a lush courtyard. Locating the main administrative functions and nursing stations in a building that faces on to two streets, we arranged five bedroom wings so as to jut out into the courtyard, giving them all views on to a tranquil green oasis. This one continuous courtyard extending between each wing actually performs the principal function of the facility, offering in-patients plenty of space to step outside for fresh air, as well as trees and flowers easily visible from any bedside window. The glazed facades combine various kinds of clear and translucent glass intermingled with opaque elements, the different qualities of filtered and reflected light helping to create a softer relationship unlike either walls or glass facades between the street and the interiors.

Hospital Cognacq-Jay in Paris

PARIS, FRANCE, 2006

This project concerns the rebuilding of 'Cognacq-Jay', a private hospital with a history of over 100 years. The site is located in the 15th district in Paris near the Eiffel Tower, within a residential quarter, home to many hospitals. The old Cognacq-Jay facilities, like many of the hospitals in this district, stood independently among the surrounding residential blocks. The main building had a T-shaped plan, and a group of small buildings and nondescript patches of garden were scattered about the site.

The international design competition to redesign the Cognacq-Jay was held in 1999 among a field of roughly 70 competitors. The programme specified an increase in beds from 72 to 168, parking space for 128 cars, new rehabilitation facilities, and a section for children suffering from various disabilities. Upgrading the quality of the medical services was a key concern of the rebuilding, in particular improvements in the hospice section. To prevent the building volume from growing unwieldy in size and organization, the requirements for each of the rooms were strictly defined in advance.

For the design, we aligned the surface lines of the exterior walls to run parallel with the streets on the north and south of the site and then placed the three hospital-ward buildings inside, maximizing the garden patios that emerge between the wards. The linear block along the street accommodates spacious gallery-type nursing rooms and private rooms arranged like apartment houses, respectively facing the street and garden, with corridors running in between. By maximizing the wall surface facing the garden, most of these private rooms are provided with views and natural lighting. Privacy inside the block, including the garden, is assured by closing the building with regard to the streets. The majority of the service functions have been collected into the first basement level, which also provides an underground link between the north and south blocks. The form of the garden with respect to the blocks allows ample sunshine and ventilation to be brought down to this level, providing a comfortable environment for the staff. We believe that these considerations play a key role in bringing the entire hospital together in a functional manner.

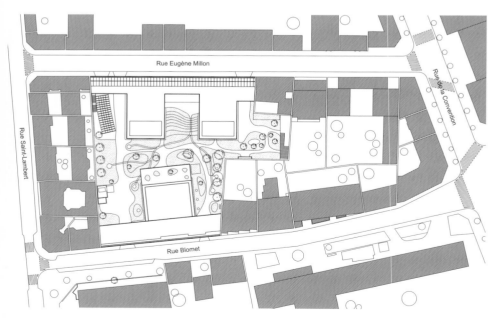

Site plan

→ View along rue Blomet

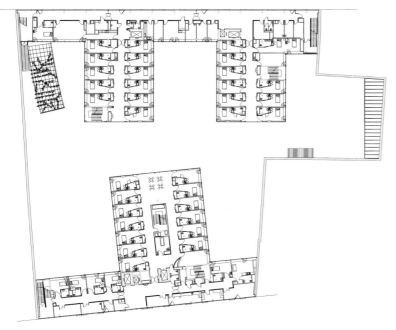

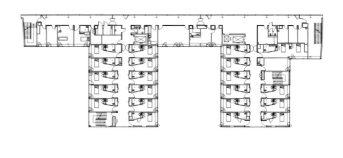

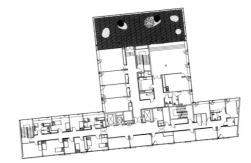

First-floor plan

Third-floor plan

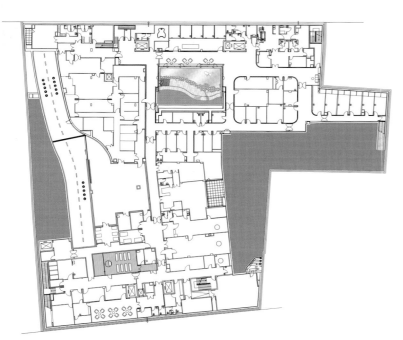

First basement floor plan

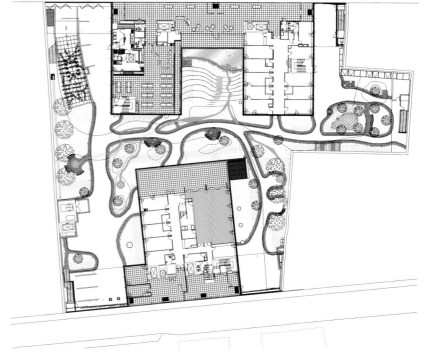

Ground floor plan

△ View from west

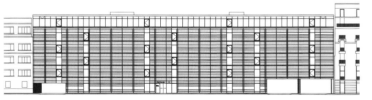

North elevation facing rue Eugene Millon

Section through courtyard

△ North wing from south
▷ View toward pond from basement lobby
← View from terrace of north wing
← Courtyard view

COMMERCIAL BUILDINGS

We designed shop buildings for two leading fashion brands in the centre of Tokyo: **TOD'S Omotesando Building** and **MIKIMOTO Ginza 2.** In recent years, both Aoyama and Ginza locations have seen considerable competition among brands wanting to build flagship boutiques, typically designed by major-name Japanese and foreign architects and constructed at costs far above that of ordinary public architecture. Perhaps the thinking is that the design of these buildings will itself establish the cultural worth of the brands. In any case, we had little experience in this field and many reservations about how to communicate with clients so very unlike public authorities. We had to propose dramatic changes to programmatic conventions, and transpose them to the realm of expression. That is, we had to bring out a major company-specific significance in the buildings. Where previously we had always pursued social values in architecture, in the world of fashion, cultural worth, indeed everything, comes down to economic value. Common to these two commercial buildings, the structural systems themselves form visual expression on the facade. In TOD'S, a network of crisscrosses forms concrete tree branches, while in MIKIMOTO, concrete is sandwiched between two steel plates and cut away in irregular shapes—a so-called 'steel-plate concrete' structure—both characteristic designs that required highly refined construction techniques to realize. In either case, our workmen had to be extremely precise in building moulds, inserting steel reinforcements and welding. Paradoxically, the more advanced the computer-aided design work and structural analyses, the more we ultimately had to rely on the skilled workmanship of the craftsmen.

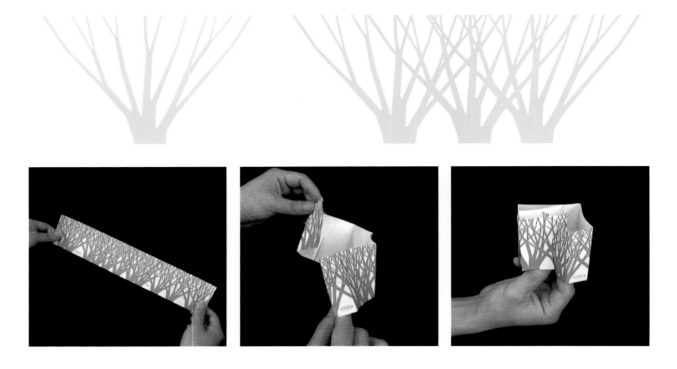

TOD'S Omotesando Building

TOKYO, 2004

Located in the fashionable Omotesando area of Tokyo, this building was built especially for TOD'S, an Italian shoe and handbag brand. The lower levels of this seven-storey building are used as a shop, with the middle and upper levels containing offices and a multipurpose space.

Since the site is L-shaped and has a narrow frontage, in order to give the building a unified volume we enclosed the site with a wall that gives the impression of a row of zelkova trees. This exterior surface serves as both graphic pattern and structural system, and is composed of 300 mm thick concrete and flush-mounted frameless glass. The resulting surface supports floor slabs spanning 10–15 metres without any internal columns.

Given the character around the site in Omotesando, where many luxury brand boutiques have been built, by selecting concrete as a material we boldly proposed a substance and strength absent from the adjacent 'glass architecture'. This concrete structure, however, is not simply used as in conventional architecture to express the volume or the massiveness of the walls. More than being merely a pattern or a structure, this building instead acquires a new dimension relating to the notion of surface.

Trees are natural objects that stand by themselves, and their shape has an inherent structural rationality. The pattern of overlapping tree silhouettes also generates a rational flow of forces. Having adapted the branched tree diagram, the higher up the building, the thinner and more numerous the branches become, with a higher ratio of openings. Similarly, the building unfolds as interior spaces with slightly different atmospheres relating to the various intended uses.

Rejecting the obvious distinctions between walls and openings, lines and planes, two and three dimensions, transparency and opaqueness, this architecture is characterized by a distinctive type of abstraction. The tree silhouette creates a new image, with a constant tension generated between the building's symbolic concreteness and its abstractness. For this project, we intended to generate a new architecture and a vivid presence for a fashion brand, with a strength that will withstand the passage of time in the cityscape.

→ Night view from Omotesando

△ Exterior view across Omotesando

← West facade

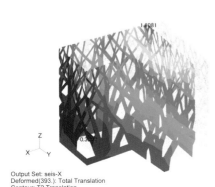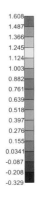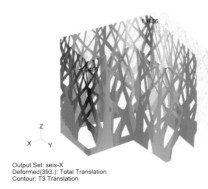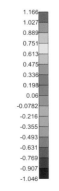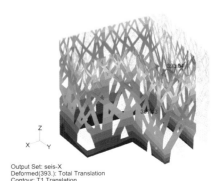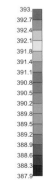

Output Set: seis-X
Deformed(393.): Total Translation
Contour: T2 Translation

Output Set: seis-X
Deformed(393.): Total Translation
Contour: T3 Translation

Output Set: seis-X
Deformed(393.): Total Translation
Contour: T1 Translation

Structural analysis of seismic loading

Fourth-floor plan

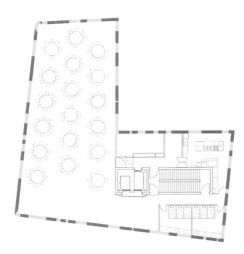

Fifth-floor plan

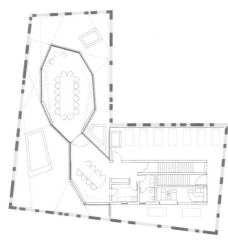

Sixth-floor plan

First-floor plan

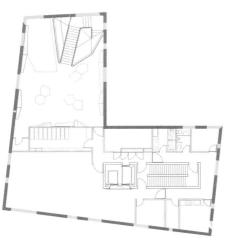

Second-floor plan

Third-floor plan

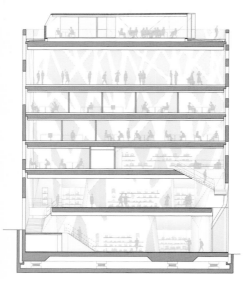

Section

Ground floor plan

Mezzanine-floor plan

△ Main stair between ground floor and first floor
▷ Second-floor shop interior

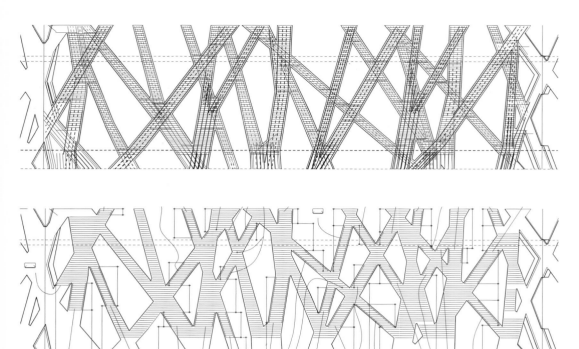

Arrangement of the exterior concrete wall

△ Sixth-floor meeting room

← Fifth-floor party space

Wall Pattern

This commercial building in Tokyo's Ginza district is designed for MIKIMOTO, a company world-famous for its pearl jewellery. The building has a 17×14 metre rectangular plan, with nine storeys above ground and one basement level. The lower level is used as a shop and offices for MIKIMOTO, and the upper floors are leased to tenants.

Our intention was to express the flow of structural forces as a design similar to the facade of TOD'S Omotesando building so as to create an impressive surface that conveys a strong presence in its surroundings. Panels composed of steel plates (6 to 12 mm in thickness) sandwiched together with studs and structural reinforcements were manufactured in a factory and conveyed to the construction site. After on-site erection and adjustment, they were welded together and 200 mm of concrete was poured inside. Through this system, in which the steel plates are treated as an expendable framework, it becomes possible to build a structure that is both extremely thin and strong. Additionally, the non-directional planar structural system allows openings to be inserted freely.

The rounded triangular and rectangular openings scattered across the metallic coated facade, are inlayed into a triangulated pattern derived from the analysis of the tectonic force flow. An image of a brilliantly scintillating gem was embodied in the cityscape of Ginza.

▽ Entrance
→ Exterior view

MIKIMOTO Ginza 2

TOKYO, JAPAN, 2005

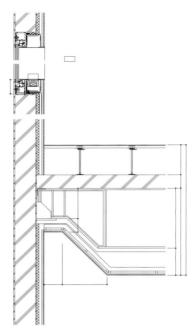

Sectional detail

Unfolded elevation

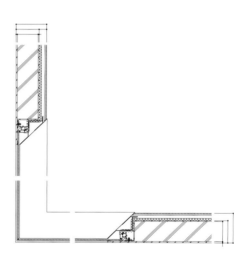

Corner detail

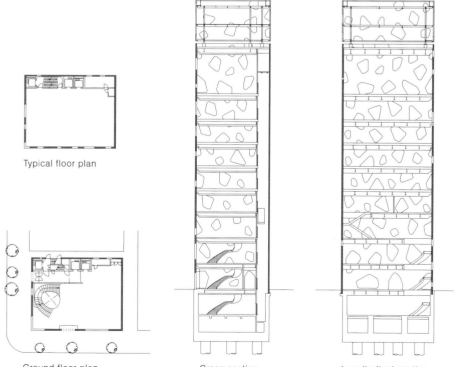

Typical floor plan

Ground floor plan

Cross section

Longitudinal section

205

△ Eighth-floor interior view
▷ Seventh-floor interior view
→ Following pages: Building in city skyline

SPIRALS

Why do so many life forms of the biosphere, plant and animal, embody spiral forms, yet architecture subsists on circles and ovals? Because, of course, buildings do not embody concepts of motion and growth. We had long wanted to incorporate spiralling geometries into our structures to realize more dynamic spaces, and finally succeeded in these two experimental projects based on spiral images: the **Relaxation Park in Torrevieja** and **Island City Central Park 'GRIN GRIN'.** For Torrevieja, we planned three large snail-shell structures. Built out of steel bars and wooden joists, the shelter looks unstable, but the interior space gives an unprecedented fluid sensation. Whereas 'GRIN GRIN' presents a series of three twisted concrete shells, the twisting manouevre turning their surfaces inside out in a rather topological gesture. These 'free-curving shells' differ from previous standard shell types that combine straight lines with spherical forms, having undergone scores of image-based free-form simulation tests and repeated partial modification in those places of greatest bending and bowing in order to achieve a certain balance. Similarly, the roof curvature of the **Meiso no Mori Municipal Funerary Hall** also comprises a series of three-dimensionally bowed free-curving shells. While derived by the same method of structural analysis as 'GRIN GRIN' it does not incorporate any spiralling geometries, hence the structure is that much more stable. As with the works in the preceding section, these projects required extremely precise handcrafting to be realized.

Relaxation Park in Torrevieja

TORREVIEJA, SPAIN, 2001–

Located in the south of Spain, Torrevieja is a resort town on the coast of the Mediterranean Sea. Blessed year round with warm sunshine and blue sky, the population of about 60,000 increases severalfold during the summer months.

Just inland from the coast are two salt lakes, which serve as symbols of the town. The water of one lake is tinged with a beautiful pink colour. The mysterious lake changes in colour from moment to moment, said to be the effect of high salt concentration and bacteria in the water. The lake water and the mud on the lakeside are beneficial in thalasso-therapy, attracting those who wish to enjoy their therapeutic benefits. The purpose of this project is to create a spa for this therapy.

The lakes and the surrounding hills form a gentle terrain. Our intention is to create a landscape like a sand dune with a gradual slope in harmony with the surrounding scenery. This is a park for relaxation, dotted with spa facilities along the contour lines. As if buried in the environment, we proposed three snail-shell-shaped buildings. The first wing has shower rooms and an office. The second building functions as a restaurant and the third a spa half exposed to the exterior, only covered by structural frames.

All of them employ the same structure to connect timber bars and steel rods drawing a spiral. Part of the exterior is enclosed with plywood, resulting in a soft exoskeleton structure similar to that of a living creature. The floors are hung from the spiral structure, and rigidity and stability are obtained by connecting the five steel rods bilaterally. Thus, all of the components perform as structural elements and generate a complete architecture.

The section takes an elliptical form, which at its largest point is approximately 12 metres wide and 9 metres high along its respective major and minor axes. The maximum floor-to-ceiling height is about 6 metres, and the longest building extends nearly 60 metres.

The landscape of the park is designed to mainly consist of the types of vegetation originally grown in this Mediterranean coast. The hope is to make this project a spacious environment where people can stroll, enjoy the shady greenery and relax by the water.

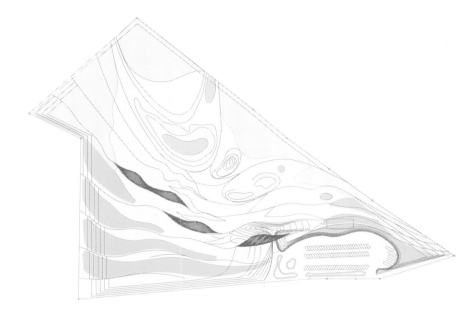

Site plan

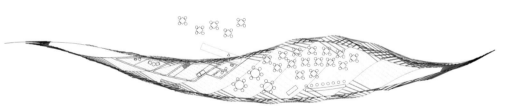

Floor plan of restaurant wing

Floor plan of information centre wing

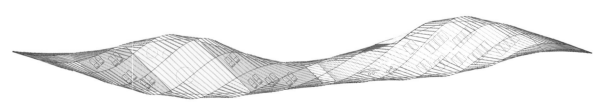

Floor plan of open air bath wing

△ Exterior view

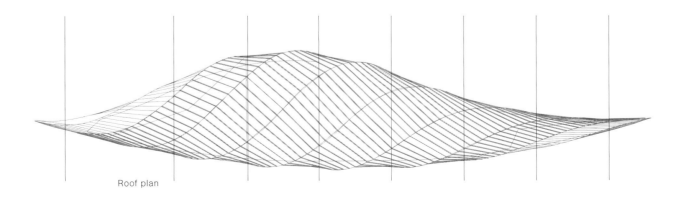

Roof plan

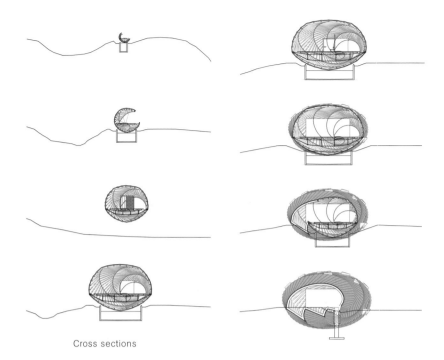

Cross sections

▽ View of exterior
→ Interior view
→ Detail of structural connection

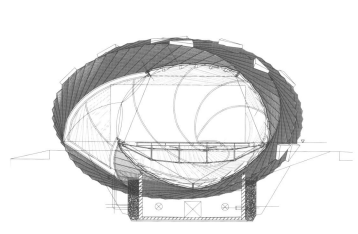

Cross section through axis

Island City is a large, roughly 400 hectare artificial island on the eastern side of Hakata Bay. The client, Fukuoka City, planned to create a new nature park on this stark and flat artificial island, and proposed a central park with a total area of 15.3 hectares and a 1.7 kilometre long green belt. The core facility of this park, named 'GRIN GRIN', is the first building on this island.

Our proposal aimed to provide a fluid and gentle change to the landscape of the whole park in order to bring various activities to the visitors.

Here, 'GRIN GRIN' is not an autonomous object, but rather an entirely new environment that merges into the topographic changes of the surrounding undulating landscape and forms a gentle spatial spiral for people to gather within. The whole landscape becomes a series of hills continuous throughout the interior and exterior where people, light and air crisscross.

The interior of this approximately 5,000 square metre complex is divided into three roughly equal spaces, each one featuring different flowers and vegetation. The northern section is a free space with the largest green area. The central section is mainly for exhibiting subtropical plants, and the south section functions as a workshop space where visitors can experience and learn how to grow plants. These three spaces are continuous with each other through the spiral form, which also generates continuity between the inside and outside. The fully planted roof top serves as a walkway that provides a sweeping view of the entire island. Here, the distinction between the ground and the roof is almost erased.

'GRIN GRIN' creates a variety of places. People can freely choose the places where they wish to sit, lie down or walk around. One could say that it is a park like a building, as well as a building like a park.

Island City Central Park 'GRIN GRIN'

FUKUOKA, 2005

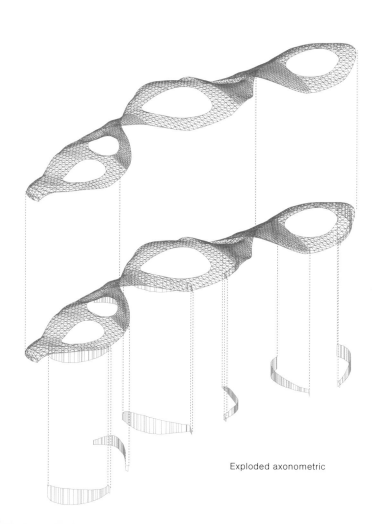

Exploded axonometric

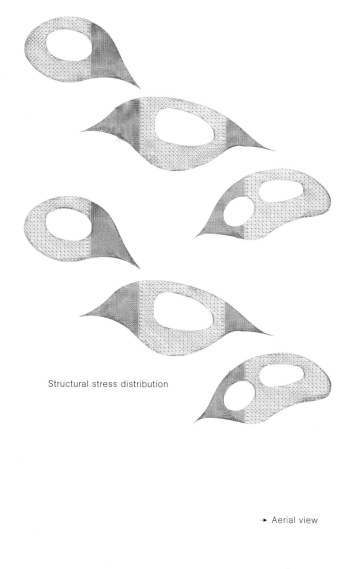

Structural stress distribution

→ Aerial view

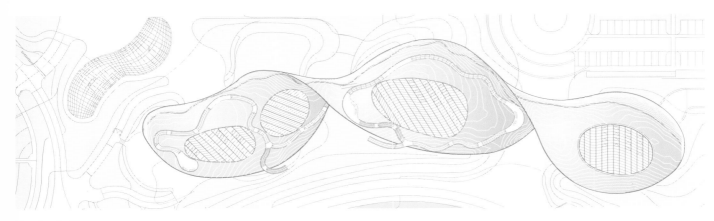

Floor level +17m

Floor level +11.7m

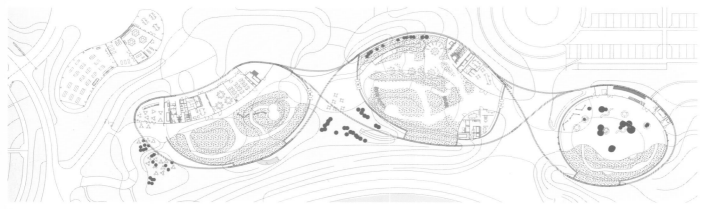

Floor level +5m

Topography. Level +4.5m

△ View of greenhouse interior
▷ Overall view from bank of pond

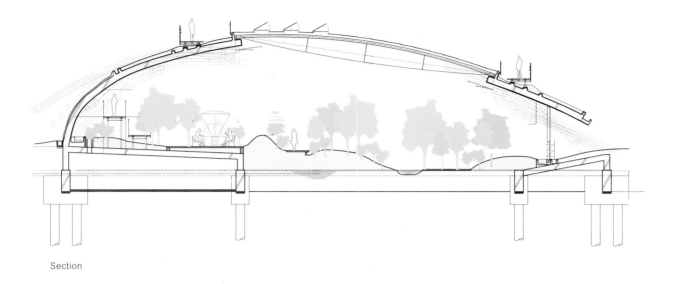

Section

△ Roof landscape
▷ Interior view beneath bridge
◄ View upward toward skylight

This is the reconstruction project of an old deteriorated crematorium in Kakamigahara, which has been planned to integrate into the surrounding park cemetery on the site. The location of the site is peaceful, facing a pond that stretches out to the north and nestled into the verdant mountains to the south.

The design brief called for a sublime space appropriate to honour the deceased, while subtly integrating into the surrounding landscape of the park cemetery. Our idea was to respond not with a conventional crematorium, but with a space formed by a roof that is like a cloud which, drifting through the sky, has come to settle upon the site, creating a pleasantly soft atmosphere. We investigated a gently curved reinforced-concrete shell structure to construct a roof characterized by concavities and convexities. The final shape of the roof structure was determined by an algorithm that generates the optimum structural solution.

Since this type of structural analysis resembles the growth patterns of plants which keep transforming, following simple natural rules, the process is called 'evolution'. After several hundred such evolutionary cycles, the optimized final shape was determined. The curved line becomes landscape, in harmony with the contours of the surrounding mountains. Four structural cores and twelve columns with built-in rainwater collection pipes are placed according to structural balance under the roof structure. Ceremonial spaces are placed between the cores and columns. The smooth curvature of the roof surface also articulates the ceiling in the interior. Indirect light softly illuminates the curved ceiling and spreads in all directions. The funeral ceremonies are held in this serene space with expressive nuances of light.

Meiso no Mori
Municipal Funeral Hall

GIFU, JAPAN, 2006

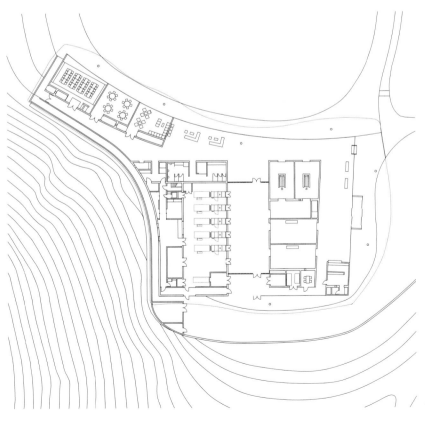

Site plan

△ View from water
▷ View from roof

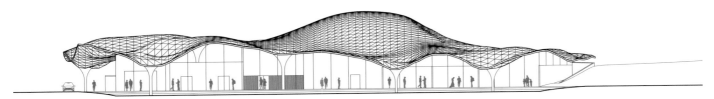

North elevation

East elevation

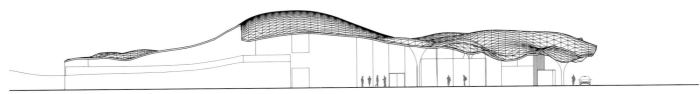

South elevation

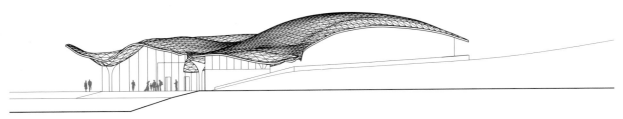

West elevation

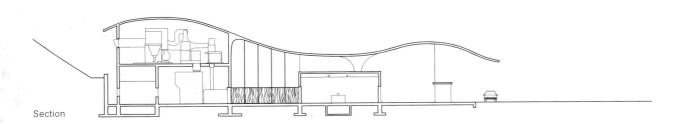

Section

△ View of roof
▷ View of entrance

△ Interior view towards pond
◁ Interior view of pre-cremation hall
→ Waiting lobby

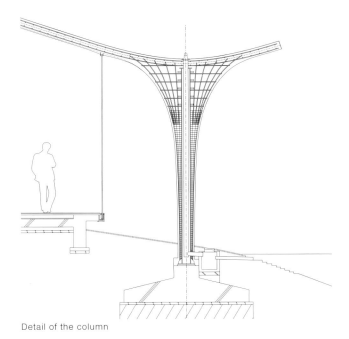

Detail of the column

→ Following pages: View from northwest

Toyo Ito: Biography

Born in 1941. After graduating from the University of Tokyo, Department of Architecture in 1965, Mr. Ito worked for the Metabolist architect Kiyonori Kikutake until 1969. In 1971 he opened his own office, Urban Robot (URBOT), which was renamed to Toyo Ito & Associates, Architects in 1979. He has taught at the University of Tokyo as a Visiting Lecturer (1988–9), at Columbia University (1991) and the University of California, Los Angeles as a Visiting Professor (1999), at Kyoto University as a Visiting Lecturer (2002–7) and at Tama Art University as a Guest Professor (2002 to the present). He also has been a commissioner of the Kumamoto Artpolis since 2005.

Publications

Transfiguration of Winds (1989, Seidosha),
Architecture in a Simulated City (1992, INAX),
Blurring Architecture (2000, Seidosha)
Michi no Ie (2006, Index Communications),
10 Adventures in the Architectural World
  (2006, Shokokusha), etc.

Awards and Prizes

Architectural Institute of Japan Prize
  (1986, for Silver Hut),
33rd Mainichi Arts Award
  (1992, for Yatsushiro Municipal Museum),
Ministry of Education Award for the
  Encouragement of Arts
  (1998, for Dome in Odate),
Japan Art Academy Prize
  (1999, for Dome in Odate),
2000 The Arnold W. Brunner Memorial Prize
  in Architecture from American Academy
  of Arts and Letters (2000),
Accorded the title 'Academician' from
  the International Academy of
  Architecture (2002),
Grand Prize of Good Design Award 2001
  from Japan Industrial Design Promotion
  Organization (2001, for Sendai
  Mediatheque),
Golden Lion for Lifetime Achievement from
  the 8th International Architecture Exhibition
  'NEXT' at the Venice Biennale (2002),
Architectural Institute of Japan Prize (2003,
  for Sendai Mediatheque),
XX ADI Compasso d'Oro Award
  (2004, for wooden bench, 'Ripples'),
Royal Gold Medal from The Royal Institute
  of British Architects (2006),
XXI ADI Compasso d'Oro Award
  (2008, for 'Stand Horm' for Milan
  Salone 2005)
6th Austrian Frederick Kiesler Prize for
  Architecture and the Arts, etc.

Projects under development

"ZA-KOENJI PUBLIC THEATRE" (Tokyo),
Taichung Metropolitan Opera House
  (Taiwan R.O.C.),
The Main Stadium for 2009 World Games
  (Taiwan R.O.C.),
National Taiwan University,
New College of Social Sciences
  (Taiwan R.O.C.),
Extension for "The Fair of Barcelona
  Gran Via Venue" (Spain),
Relaxation Park in Torrevieja (Spain),
University of California, Berkeley Art Museum
  and Pacific Film Archive (U.S.A.), etc.

Project Data

White U
Location / dates: Honcho, Nakano-ku, Tokyo, Japan / 1975.9–1976.5
Structure: reinforced concrete / 1 storey
Site area / building area / total floor area: 367.61m² / 150.97m² / 148.25m²
Structural Engineer: Minoru Tanaka
Mechanical Engineer: Masamitsu Kaizuka

House in Kasama
Location / dates: Shimoichige, Kasama-shi, Ibaraki, Japan / 1980.9–1981.11
Structure: wood frame / 2 storeys
Site area / building area / total floor area: 865.48m² / 155.24m² / 289.91m²
Furniture Design: Teruaki Ohashi

Silver Hut
Location / dates: Honcho, Nakano-ku, Tokyo, Japan / 1982.10–1984.7
Structure: reinforced concrete, steel frame / 2 storeys
Site area / building area / total floor area: 403.46m² / 119.99m² / 138.81m²
Structural Engineers: Gengo Matsui + O.R.S.
Mechanical Engineers: Yamazaki Electric Engineering
Furniture Design: Teruaki Ohashi

House in Magomezawa
Location / dates: Magome-cho, Funabashi-shi, Chiba, Japan / 1985.5–1986.5
Structure: reinforced concrete, steel frame / 2 storeys
Site area / building area / total floor area: 100.00m² / 49.65m² / 81.18m²
Structural Engineers: Gengo Matsui + O.R.S.

Tower of Winds in Yokohama
Location / dates: Kitasaiwai, Nishi-ku, Yokohama-shi, Kanagawa, Japan / 1986.3–1986.11
Structure: steel frame
Building area: 43.45m²
Structural Engineers: Gengo Matsui + O.R.S.
Collaborator: T.L. Yamagiwa

Egg of Winds
Location / dates: Tsukuda, Chuo-ku, Tokyo, Japan / 1988.4–1991.3
Structure: steel frame
Building area: 118.53m²
Structural Engineers: Katsuo Nakata & Associates + Taisei Corporation
Mechanical Engineers: Taisei Corporation

Restaurant Bar "Nomad"
Location / dates: Roppongi, Minato-ku, Tokyo, Japan / 1986.1–1986.8
Structure: steel frame / 3 storeys
Site area / building area / total floor area: 332.84m² / 271.00m² / 427.47m²
Structural Engineers: Gengo Matsui + O.R.S.
Mechanical Engineers: Kawaguchi Mechanical Engineering and Yamazaki Electric Engineering

ITM Building in Matsuyama
Location / dates: Higashiisiimachi, Matsuyama-shi, Ehime, Japan / 1991.5–1993.1
Structure: steel frame / 3 storeys
Site area / building area / total floor area: 831.66m² / 486.37m² / 1,255.68m²
Structural Engineers: Toshihiko Kimura + Structural Design Office Oak
Mechanical Engineers: Kawaguchi Mechanical Engineering and Yamazaki Electric Engineering

T Building in Nakameguro
Location / dates: Higashiyama, Meguro-ku, Tokyo, Japan / 1989.4–1990.5
Structure: steel frame, reinforced concrete / 3 storeys, 1 basement, 1 penthouse
Site area / building area / total floor area: 584.05m² / 401.57m² / 1,443.77m²
Structural Engineers: Katsuo Nakata
Mechanical Engineers: Kawaguchi Mechanical Engineering and Yamazaki Electric Engineering

Yatsushiro Municipal Museum
Location / dates: Nishimatsuejomachi, Yatsushiro-shi, Kumamoto, Japan / 1988.10–1991.3
Structure: reinforced concrete, steel frame / 4 storeys, 1 basement
Site area / building area / total floor area: 8,223.20m² / 1,432.88m² / 3,418.30m²
Structural Engineers: Kimura Structural Engineers
Mechanical Engineers: Uichi Inoue Research Installation
Furniture Design: Teruaki Ohashi

Gallery U in Yugawara
Location / dates: Yugawaramachi, Ashigarashimo-gun, Kanagawa, Japan / 1989.7–1991.5
Structure: reinforced concrete, steel frame / 2 storeys
Site area / building area / total floor area: 1,275.73m² / 261.70m² / 256.26m²
Structural Engineers: Kimura Structural Engineers
Mechanical Engineers: Uichi Inoue Research Installation

Shimosuwa Municipal Museum
Location / dates: Nisitakagi, Shimosuwa-cho, Suwa-gun, Nagano, Japan / 1990.4–1993.3
Structure: reinforced concrete, steel frame / 2 storeys
Site area/building area / total floor area: 5,277.55m² / 1,369.99m² / 1,982.78m²
Structural Engineers: Toshihiko Kimura + Matsumoto Structural Design
Mechanical Engineers: Tetens Engineering Co., Ltd., and Setsubi Keikaku Co., Ltd.

Home for the Elderly in Yatsushiro

Location / dates: Hinaguheiseimachi, Yatsushiro-shi, Kumamoto, Japan / 1992.10 – 1994.3
Structure: reinforced concrete, steel frame / 2 storeys
Site area / building area / total floor area: 7,425m² / 1,827.70m² / 2,487.10m²
Structural Engineers: Toshihiko Kimura + Matsumoto Structural Design
Mechanical Engineers: Uichi Inoue Research Installation, Ohtaki E&M Consultant and N.E. Planners Inc.

Yatsushiro Fire Station

Location / dates: Omuramachi Yatsushiro-shi, Kumamoto, Japan / 1992.4 – 1995.3
Structure: steel frame / 2 storeys, 1 basement (main training wing, 5 storeys)
Site area / building area / total floor area: 8,055.44m² / 3,225.81m² / 4,683.92m²
Structural Engineers: Kimura Structural Engineers
Mechanical Engineers: Uichi Inoue Research Installation, Ohtaki E&M Consultant and N.E. Planners Inc.

Odate Jukai Dome

Location / dates: Kamidaino, Odate-shi, Akita, Japan / 1993.10–1997.6
Structure: wood frame, steel frame / 2 storeys
Site area/building area / total floor area: 110,250.67m² / 21,910.65m² + 1,792.88m²
Architectural Design: Toyo Ito & Associates, Architects + Takenaka Corporation
Structural Engineers: Takenaka Corporation
Mechanical Engineers: Takenaka Corporation

Nagaoka Lyric Hall

Location / dates: Terajimamachi, Nagaoka-shi, Niigata, Japan / 1993.4 – 1996.10
Structure: reinforced concrete, steel frame / 4 storeys
Site area / building area / total floor area: 39,700.00m² / 6,682.38m² / 9,708.13m²
Structural Engineers: Toshihiko Kimura + Hanawa Structural Engineers Co., Ltd.
Mechanical Engineers: Uichi Inoue Laboratory, Setsubi Keikaku Co., Ltd.
Acoustic Engineers: Nagata Acoustics
Theater Design: Shozo Motosugi
Landscape Design: Mikiko Ishikawa + Tokyo Landscape Architects

T Hall in Shimane

Location / dates: Taishacho, Hikawa-gun, Shimane, Japan / 1996.5 – 1999.7
Structure: reinforced concrete, steel frame / 4 storeys
Site area / building area / total floor area: 20,400.17m² / 5,567.37m² / 5,847.36m²
Structural Engineers: Toshihiko Kimura + Sasaki Structural Consultants
Mechanical Engineers: Sogo Consultants
Acoustic Engineers: Nagata Acoustics
Theater Design: Shozo Motosugi

Matsumoto Performing Arts Centre

Location/dates: Fukashi, Matsumoto-shi, Nagano, Japan / 2000.11 – 2004.3
Structure: steel framed reinforced concrete, steel frame / 7 storeys, 2 basement levels, 1 penthouse
Site area / building area / total floor area: 9,142.50m² / 7,080.02m² / 19,184.38m²
Structural Engineers: Sasaki Structural Consultants
Mechanical Engineers: Kankyo Engineering Inc.
Acoustic Engineers: Nagata Acoustics
Lighting Design: LIGHTDESIGN
Landscape Design: Mikiko Ishikawa + Tokyo Landscape Architects

Sendai Mediatheque

Location / dates: Kasugamachi, Aoba-ku, Sendai-shi, Miyagi, Japan / 1995.4 – 2000.8
Structure: steel frame, reinforced concrete / 7 storeys, 2 basement levels
Site area / building area / total floor area: 3,948.72m² / 2,933.12m² / 21,682.15m²
Structural Engineers: Sasaki Structural Consultants
Mechanical Engineers: ES Associates, Sogo Consultants, Otaki E&M Consultants
Lighting Design: Lighting Planners Associates Inc.

Tama Art University Library (Hachioji Campus)

Location / dates: Hachioji City, Tokyo, Japan / 2004.4 – 2007.2
Structure: steel+concrete mixed structure, reinforced concrete construction (basement) / 2 storeys, 1 basement
Site area / building area / total floor area: 159,184.87m² / 2,224.59m² / 5,639.46m²
Campus Planning: Tama Art University Campus Project Team
Structural Engineers: Sasaki Structural Consultants
Associate Architects (Architectural, Structural and Mechanical Design): Kajima Design
Interaction Design: Workshop for Architecture and Urbanism
Furniture Design: Fujie Kazuko Atelier

Bruges Pavilion

Location / dates: Bruges, Belgium / 2000.4 – 2002.2
Structure: aluminium structure / 1 storey
Building area: 96.60m²
Structural Engineers: Structural Design Office Oak Inc.
Management: bdp- Hera van Sande

Serpentine Gallery Pavilion 2002

Location / dates: Kensington Gardens, London, UK / 2002.1 – 2002.7
Structure: steel frame / 1 storey
Building area / total floor area: 309.76m² / 309.76m²
Architectural Design: Toyo Ito and Cecil Balmond (Arup)
Structural Engineers: Arup
Mechanical Engineers: Arup

Aluminium Cottage

Location / dates: Nanbucho, Minamikoma-gun, Yamanashi, Japan / 2002.6 – 2004.8
Structure: aluminium structure / 2 storeys
Site area / building area / total floor area: 8,300m² / 57.42m² / 74.44m²
Structural Engineers: Structural Design Office Oak Inc.
Mechanical Engineers: ES Associates

Aluminium Brick Housing in Groningen

Location / dates: Groningen, Netherlands / 2001.3 – 2005.1
Structure: aluminium structure / 3 storeys
Site area / building area / total floor area: 163.6m² / 150.3m² / 361.9m²
Collaborating Architects: Hosoya Schaefer Architects
Collaborating Architects (Netherlands): KAW architecten Studio Sputnik
Structural Engineers: Structural Design Office Oak Inc.

Dormitory for SUS Company Fukushima Branch

Location / dates: Nijinodai, Sukagawa-shi, Fukushima, Japan / 2004.4 – 2005.9
Structure: aluminium structure / 1 storey
Site area / building area / total floor area: 1,566.55m² / 489.20m² / 489.20m²
Structural Engineers: Structural Design Office Oak Inc.
Mechanical Engineers: Kankyo Engineering Inc.

Hospital Cognacq-Jay in Paris

Location / dates: Paris, France / 1999.10 – 2006.9
Structure: reinforced concrete, steel frame / 6 storeys, 2 basement levels
Site area / building area / total floor area: 4,976m² / 3,207m² / 17,968m²
Collaborating Architects (Japan): Jun Yanagisawa (Contemporaries), Manuel Tardits (MIKAN)
Collaborating Architects (France): Extra Muros
Structural Engineers: SAPS / Sasaki and Partners (Japan), Setec (France)
Mechanical Engineers: Kankyo Engineering Inc. (Japan), Setec (France)
Facade Design Consultants: R.F.R (France)

TOD'S Omotesando Building

Location / dates: Jingumae, Shibuya-ku, Tokyo, Japan / 2002.4 – 2004.11
Structure: reinforced concrete, steel frame / 7 storeys, 1 basement
Site area / building area / total floor area: 516.23m² / 401.55m² / 2,548.84m²
Structural Engineers: Structural Design Office OAK Inc.
Mechanical Engineers: ES Associates

MIKIMOTO Ginza 2

Location / dates: Ginza, Chuuo-ku, Tokyo, Japan / 2003.8 – 2005.11
Structure: steel frame and concrete, reinforced concrete / 9 storeys, 1 basement
Site area / building area / total floor area: 275.74m² / 237.69m² / 2,205.02m²
Architectural Design: Toyo Ito & Associates, Architects + TAISEI DESIGN PAE
Structural Engineers: Sasaki Structural Consultants + TAISEI DESIGN PAE
Mechanical Engineers: TAISEI DESIGN PAE

Relaxation Park in Torrevieja

Location / dates: Torrevieja (Alicante), Spain / 2001.4–
Structure: steel frame, wood frame / 1 storey
Site area / building area / total floor area: 8ha / 431m² (total 1,599m²) / 349m² (total 1,249m²)
Collaborating Architects (Japan): Kenichi Shinozaki
Collaborating Architects (Spain): Jose Maria Torres Nadal, Antonio Marqueríe Tamayo, Joaquin Alvado Bañón
Structural Engineers: SAPS/Sasaki & Partners + Masahiro Ikeda Architecture Studio, Obiol & Moya Arquitectes Associates (First phase), Salvador Perez Arroyo (Second phase)
Mechanical Engineers: Kankyo Engineering Inc. (Japan), Fernando Lamas (Spain)

Island City Central Park 'GRIN GRIN'

Location / dates: Kashiihama, Higashi-ku, Fukuoka-shi, Fukuoka, Japan / 2002.10 – 2005.4
Structure: reinforced concrete, steel frame / 1 storey
Site area / building area / total floor area: 129,170.00m² / 5,162.07m² / 5,033.47m²
Structural Engineers: Sasaki Structural Consultants
Mechanical Engineers: Kankyo Engineering Inc.
Landscape Design: Sohgoh Landspape Planning Office

Meiso no Mori Municipal Funerary Hall

Location / dates: Nakaoogihira, Kakamigahara-shi, Gifu, Japan / 2004.5 – 2006.5
Structure: reinforced concrete / 2 storeys
Site area/building area / total floor area: 6,695.97m² / 2,269.66m² / 2,264.57m²
Structural Engineers: Sasaki Structural Consultants
Mechanical Engineers: Kankyo Engineering Inc.
Landscape Design: Mikiko Ishikawa

...ita, Odate Jukai Dome 32, 103, 104, *104–9*
Alessi, dishware 25
Aluminium Brick Housing, Groningen 167, 172,
    172–75
Aluminium Cottage, Yamanashi
    167, 168, *168–71*
Aluminium House 28
Amsterdam, Mahler 4, Block 5 22
Araya, Masato 23, 157
Art Nouveau 27–8
Asada, Akira, and Taro Igarashi,
    playing card images *24*, 25

Balmond, Cecil 21, 23, 157, 162
Barcelona, Gran Via Trade Fair campus 21
Benjamin, Walter 28
Branzi, Andrea 21
Bruges Pavilion, Bruges 21, 23, 157, 158,
    158–61
Buntrock, Dana 21–5

Chiba, House in Magomezawa 45, 52, *52–5*
Coimbra, Santa Cruz Park 29

Dormitory for SUS Corporation Fukushima
    Branch, Fukushima 167, 176, *176–83*
Dunne, Anthony 23

Egg of Winds, Tokyo 57, 62, *62–3*
Ehime, ITM Building in Matsuyama 69, 70, *70–3*
Eiffel, Gustave 27

Frampton, Kenneth 22, 25
Frankfurt Opera House, lighting 22
Fujimori, Terunobu 26, *27*
Fukuoka, Island City Central Park
    'GRIN GRIN' 9, 23, 29, 209, 215, *215–9*
Fukushima, Dormitory for SUS Corporation
    Fukushima Branch 167, 176, *176–83*

Gallery U in Yugawara, Kanagawa 79, 84, *84–7*
Gaudí, Antonio, 27, 28
Ghent Forum for Music, Dance and Visual Culture
    21, 22
Gifu, Meiso no Mori Municipal Funeral Hall 9, 22,
    23, 209, 220, *220–7*
'GRIN GRIN', Island City Central Park, Fukuoka
    23, 29, 209, 215, *215–9*
Groningen, Aluminium Brick Housing 167, 172,
    172–75

Hatakeyama, Naoya 21
Herron, Ron 22
Heuser, Michael 26
Home for the Elderly in Yatsushiro,
    Kumamoto 93, 94, *94–7*
Hospital Cognacq-Jay, Paris 185, 186, *186–91*
House in Kasama, Kasama 28, 35, 40, *40–3*
House in Magomezawa, Chiba 45, 52, *52–5*

Igarashi, Taro 26-9
Igarashi, Taro and Akira Asada, playing card
    images *24*, 25
Island City Central Park 'GRIN GRIN', Fukuoka 9,
    23, 29, 209, 215, *215–9*
Isozaki, Arata 23, 79, 80
ITM Building in Matsuyama, Ehime 69, 70, *70–3*

Jencks, Charles 22

Kanagawa, Gallery U in Yugawara 79, 84, *84–7*
Kanagawa, Tower of Winds in Yokohama 22, 28,
    32, 57, 58, *58–61*, 88
Kasama, House in Kasama 28, 35, 40, *40–3*
Kikutake, Kiyonori 29, 30–1, 32
Koolhaas, Rem 26
Kumamoto Art Polis 79, 80
Kumamoto, Home for the Elderly in
    Yatsushiro 93, 94, *94–7*
Kumamoto, Yatsushiro Fire Station 93, 98,
    98–101
Kumamoto, Yatsushiro Municipal Museum 23,
    28, 32, 79, 80, *80–3*, *88*, 93

Le Corbusier 93
London, Serpentine Gallery Pavilion 2002 9, 21,
    25, 29, 156, 162, *162–5*

Mahler 4, Block 5, Amsterdam 22
Maison de la culture du Japon à Paris 69
Marriage of Figaro, stage sets 22
Matsumoto Performing Arts Centre, Nagano
    9, 23, 24, 26, 111, 122, *122–31*
Max Protech Gallery 25
Meiso no Mori Municipal Funeral Hall, Gifu 9, 22,
    23, 209, 220, *220–7*
MIKIMOTO Ginza 2, Tokyo 9, 22, 23, 156, 193,
    202, *202–7*
Miyagi, Sendai Mediatheque 9, 21, 22, 23, 24–5,
    27–8, 29, *32*, 32–3, 69, 131, 134, *134–43*

Nagano, Matsumoto Performing Arts Centre 9,
    23, 24, 26, 111, 122, *122–31*
Nagano, Shimosuwa Municipal Museum 79, 88,
    88–91
Nagaoka Lyric Hall, Niigata 111, 112, *112–15*
Nakono, White U 31–2
Nederlands Architectuurinstituut, Rotterdam 27
'The New "*Real*" in Architecture' 29
Niigata, Nagaoka Lyric Hall 111, 112, *112–15*

Odate Jukai Dome, Akita 32, 103, 104, *104–9*
Okawabata River City 62
Omiwatari 26
Onbashira Festival 26
Osaka Expo 23

'Pao for the Tokyo Nomad Women' 28
Pao II (Brussels 1989) 21
Paris, Hospital Cognacq-Jay 185, 186, *186–91*
Paxton, Joseph 27

Relaxation Park, Torrevieja 23, 208, 210, *210–13*
Restaurant Bar 'Nomad', Tokyo 25, 57, 64, *64–7*

Sasaki, Mutsuro 21
Sejima, Kazuyo 29
S Project in Scotland 23
Sendai Mediatheque, Miyagi 9, 21, 22, 23, 24–5,
    27–8, 29, *32*, 32–3, 69, 131, 134, *134–43*
Serpentine Gallery Pavilion 2002, London 9, 21,
    25, 29, 156, 162, *162–5*
Shimane, T Hall 111, 116, *116–9*
Shimosuwa Municipal Museum, Nagano 79, 88,
    88–91
Shinohara, Kazuo 30–2
Silver Hut, Tokyo 28, 32, 45, 46, *46–51*, 79
Singapore, VivoCity 23
Smithson, Robert 26
Suwako Museum 26

T Building in Nakameguro, Tokyo 69, 70, 74,
    74–7
T Hall, Shimane 111, 116, *116–19*
Taichung Metropolitan Opera House, Taiwan 21,
    22, 29
Taki, Koji 25, 31
Takiguchi, Noriko 26
Tama Art University Library (Hachioji Campus),
    Tokyo 23, 25, 29, 133, 144, *144–55*
Tange, Kenzo 29
TOD'S Omotesando Building, Tokyo 9, 23, 29,
    157, 193, 194, *194–201*, 202
Tokyo, Egg of Winds 57, 62, *62–3*
Tokyo, MIKIMOTO Ginza 2 9, 22, 23, 156, 193,
    202, *202–7*
Tokyo, Restaurant Bar 'Nomad' 25, 57, 64, *64–7*
Tokyo, Silver Hut 28, 32, 45, 46, *46–51*, 79
Tokyo, Tama Art University Library (Hachioji
    Campus) 23, 25, 29, 133, 144, *144–55*
Tokyo, T Building in Nakameguro 69, 70, 74,
    74–7
Tokyo, TOD'S Omotesando Building 9, 23, 29,
    157, 193, 194, *194–201*, 202
Tokyo, White U 9, 25, 28, 31–2, 35, 36, *36–9*,
    40, 45, *47*
Torres, Elias 23, *23*
Torrevieja, Relaxation Park 23, 208, 210, *210–23*
Tower of Winds in Yokohama, Kanagawa 22, 28,
    32, 57, 58, *58–61*, 88
Tsukio, Yoshio 23

University of California, Berkeley Art Museum and
    Pacific Film Archive 22

'Visions of Japan' (London, 1991) 22, 23, 25
VivoCity, Singapore 23

White U, Tokyo 9, 25, 28, 31–2, 35, 36, *36–9*,
    40, 45, *47*

Yamamoto, Riken 30–3
Yamanashi, Aluminium Cottage 167, 168, *168–71*
Yatsushiro Fire Station, Kumamoto 93, 98,
    98–101
Yatsushiro Municipal Museum, Kumamoto 23,
    28, 32, 79, 80, *80–3*, *88*, 93

Picture Credits

Phaidon Press Limited
Regent's Wharf
All Saints Street
London N1 9PA

Phaidon Press Inc.
180 Varick Street
New York, NY 10014

www.phaidon.com

First published 2009
© 2009 Phaidon Press Limited

ISBN 978 0 7148 4505 0

A CIP catalogue record for
this book is available from the
British Library

Designed by
Heimann und Schwantes, Berlin

Printed in China